NORDIC
HOMES in
COLOUR

NORDIC
HOMES in
COLOUR

THE NEW SCANDI STYLE

ANTONIA AF PETERSENS

Photography by
BETH EVANS

RYLAND PETERS & SMALL
LONDON • NEW YORK

Senior designer Toni Kay
Senior commissioning editor
  Annabel Morgan
Location research Jess Walton
Head of Production
  Patricia Harrington
Creative director Leslie Harrington
Publisher Cindy Richards

Styling Sania Pell

First published in 2017 as
New Nordic Colour. This
edition published in 2024
by Ryland Peters & Small
20–21 Jockey's Fields,
London WC1R 4BW
and
341 East 116th Street
New York, NY 10029

www.rylandpeters.com

Text copyright © Antonia
af Petersens 2017, 2024
Design and photographs copyright
© Ryland Peters & Small 2017, 2024

10 9 8 7 6 5 4 3 2 1

ISBN 978-1-78879-592-0

A CIP record for this book is available
from the British Library.

Library of Congress CIP data has been
applied for.

Printed and bound in China

FSC
www.fsc.org
MIX
Paper from
responsible sources
FSC® C106563

CONTENTS

INTRODUCTION

To many of us, the term 'Nordic colour' may seem like something of a contradiction in terms. The quintessential Nordic home is not known for its vibrant use of colour. Instead, the classic Scandi look, as seen in interiors magazines and Nordic Noir TV series, boasts white walls, white floors, black-framed windows, tasteful black and white prints on the walls and a smattering of leafy houseplants.

The geographical position of the Nordic region results in striking seasonal variations – long days that stretch into light evenings in the summer, and almost never-ending darkness and extreme cold during the autumn and winter months. Unsurprisingly, the meteorological conditions dictate how people work, play and live in the region, and the scant daylight during the winter is the main reason that Scandinavians constantly seek light, brightness and warmth.

However, in recent years something has changed. The Nordic colour palette is slowly moving away from cool whites and pale greys, and stronger, bolder hues are making an appearance in Nordic homes. The common denominator is that white walls have been replaced with bold colourful shades, but it is possible to determine three different strands within this new approach.

The first style I have dubbed Dark Eclectic. Perhaps as a reaction to spacious, pared-down, white, bright interiors, Dark Eclectic is typified by a use of deep, intense hues: dusk blue, storm grey and forest green, inspired by the dramatic tones of the Nordic landscape. Leafy plants and natural materials – wood, leather, straw – combined with eclectic details all come together to create a well-balanced interior that is shown to best advantage against a dark background.

The next style, Bold Accents, provides variety and choice. Pale walls may remain in some homes, yet they are enlivened by vivid, striking accents in the shape of decorative detailing, colourful kitchen cabinets and bold furniture. This style embraces brave details that stand out and add character to an interior.

Lastly, we will focus on a lighter interpretation of Nordic colour in the form of Majestic Pastels. This look is not so much about delicate sugared-almond hues but instead focuses on strong, sophisticated pastel shades with a fresh, bold feel.

Why did Scandinavians suddenly start to welcome colour, and how is it being used? In this book we will dive deep into the phenomenon of *Nordic Homes in Colour* and learn how to embrace modern colour the Scandinavian way.

WHAT IS THE
NEW NORDIC
COLOUR?

THE STORY OF NORDIC COLOUR

There is a popular belief that Nordic interiors have always been light, bright and white. But the pale, walls and minimalist interiors that have dominated Scandinavian homes in recent years have their roots in a style that emerged in the last century.

In reality, many design movements have influenced the region's interiors over the centuries and the new Nordic use of colour is not really new at all, at least not if we take a closer look at how colour has been used in this region in the past.

The white, minimalist interiors so typical of Scandinavian homes in the past few decades date back to the Stockholm Exhibition of 1930, which established functionalism as the dominant style in the Nordic region. The exhibition showcased

a modernist lifestyle, with model housing boasting pared-down furnishings, large windows and clean white walls – a seductive vision of contemporary living.

After the Second World War, the term 'Scandinavian Modern' was coined by the Anglo-American design world in the 1950s. The style emerged via several exhibitions featuring design from Nordic countries and the establishment of Scandinavian design as a commodity put names such as Alvar Aalto, Hans J Wegner, Bruno Mathsson and Finn Juhl on the map and paved the way for manufacturers to produce 'products for good living'. Scandinavian Modern interiors were cultured and restrained, with pale walls, natural wood and beautiful, functional furniture. It was around this time that Scandinavian interiors became synonymous with good taste, and the stereotype has persisted ever since.

But modernism is only one side of the story. The Baroque period featured gold accents and rich hues while in 18th-century Sweden the Gustavian style espoused elegantly muted pastels. The Arts and Crafts movement that developed in England during the late 19th century spread to the Nordic region, bringing with it a colour palette of natural pigments: earthy brown, forest green, poppy red and deep plum.

During the 1920s, the Swedish Grace movement was famous for its playful Neoclassical style and subdued Art Deco hues. And we only need to rewind a few decades to find colourful walls in Nordic homes. In the 1970s, Scandinavians painted and papered with strong colours and bold patterns. The 1980s saw a revival of the Gustavian style and a sophisticated palette of pale pink, sky blue and apricot. The 1990s turned to earthy natural tones such as terracotta, cobalt blue and pistachio green, before colours once again lightened, and turned slowly to white, grey and beige.

So the concept of Nordic colour is not exactly a new one. But, as this book will reveal, after a long period of neutral colour and minimal decor, we are currently witnessing a new and exciting infusion of bold, beautiful and refreshing colour.

EMBRACING NEW NORDIC COLOUR

A look in the rear-view mirror proves that history always repeats itself. Trends are cyclical and, believe it or not, what's on trend today will look decidedly passé five or ten years down the line.

When it comes to new trends, the fashion industry is the first to react, but the interior decoration and design industry is never far behind. New technology and social media have made the tempo faster, which, in turn, makes trend cycles shorter. Trends often represent a reaction to what has gone before, but they are also affected by politics, societal movements and changing demographics.

When it comes to colour, the theory is that trends repeat in cycles of 10–15 years. When our surroundings are white and neutral, we grow bored after a while and start to move towards the other end of the spectrum, and that pattern is evident in interior design over the centuries. In the last 15 years, neutral colours such as white and grey have dominated Scandinavian homes. But, in tune with the trend cycle, the palette is changing. At Nordic design expositions and fairs, interior design is gravitating towards clearer, stronger colours — orange, pink, red and even brown. And this shift is likely to be a reaction to the recent dominance of minimalist white.

We will see this new trend for colour taking hold internationally, but Nordic homes are early adopters. Given their geographical, social and cultural environment, Swedes, Danes, Norwegians and Finns are able to carry out extensive home redecoration, since they not only have the desire but also the means to do so. As colour trends start to develop, Scandinavians have been swift to embrace them.

NEUTRALS

The two non-chromatic elementary colours are white and black, with the popular greyscale in between them. Even though it may not seem like it, white is a colour and comes in a variety of shades. Yellow undertones create a warmer, creamier white, while those with blue undertones are crisper and colder. Among Swedes, the search for the perfect white paint has resulted in the term 'Stockholm White' — a white colour with subtle yellow and grey undertones that has become synonymous with standard white.

White and pale greys go nicely with both hot and cold hues, and make an ideal backdrop if you want to let your possessions play a starring role. Mid-greys create a soft, moody feel and are versatile. The Nordic landscape harmonizes with grey most of the year, so it is possible to find inspiration outdoors — think of freshly fallen snow, cloud cover or frozen lakes.

BLUE AND GREEN

As the trend cycle slowly moves from white to grey to colour, blue and green shades are often the first step on the way. Recently, darker and greener greys have increased in popularity and a dark petrol blue shade reminiscent of inland lakes has also appeared.

Green and blue are colours that remind us of the landscape — sky, sea, grassy fields, woods — and they are also excellent accents. The blue palette is incredibly comprehensive, ranging from violet, with red undertones, to green shades via turquoise. In Scandinavia, there is a new interest in deep, subdued tones such as airforce blue and navy.

Green is produced by mixing blue and yellow, and its character changes depending on how much of each is used in the mixing process. It evokes a sense of calm and serenity, and is therefore a popular choice for bedrooms. In Scandinavia, green hues are mainly represented by grey-green tones with lots of white or black in them. Think of sage, moss green or khaki, forest green and seaweed.

RED AND YELLOW

As we move around the colour wheel, we eventually come to hot colours such as red and yellow. Scandinavians tend to be attracted to blackened or muted versions of these shades and, as with blue and green, dirtier shades have proved popular in the transition from white to colour. Powdery pink, for example, is seen a lot, often with putty undertones that prevent it from being too sugary sweet. Bold, deep red tones are also popular but they are not vibrant, instead flirting with natural reds such as lingonberry, rust and terracotta.

In the middle of the red-yellow tonality we find orange hues. These warm colours bring mustard, clay and earth to mind — hues that are not traditionally associated with Scandinavia, but which in recent years have become more popular.

Bright red is dramatic and intense and therefore suitable for social spaces such as living rooms or dining rooms. Yellow, on the other hand, is a refreshing colour that provides warmth and is cheerful and optimistic. Both colours are perfect used as accents as well as colour blocks.

DARK NEUTRALS

Research within colour psychology predicts that chromatic or strongly pigmented colours grow darker and moodier as the trend cycle moves towards dark neutrals such as charcoal and mahogany. In the same way as white, black makes a perfect understated backdrop. Mixing black with small amounts of red creates a warmer black that is easy to live with.

After the recent craze for all shades of grey, there is a new interest in warm, dark brown hues. Experiment with shades of chocolate, rust, coffee or bark, and use your favourite hue to paint an entire room or just one wall. Dark walls create depth and make accents and luxurious materials stand out.

THE NORDIC
WAY WITH
COLOUR

DARK ECLECTIC

Perhaps the most popular new Nordic palette is one that I have dubbed Dark Eclectic. It represents a reaction against the bright, white-painted spaces that we associate with Scandinavian style; pale hues have been replaced by darker colours such as storm grey, forest green and indigo.

Nature is a huge source of interior inspiration in Scandinavia, perhaps now more than ever. Increasingly crowded cities and a rapid rate of urbanization have led to a yearning for the natural environment and these desires are reflected in interior trends that embrace natural colours, textures and materials.

The 'eclectic' part of this style is something of a backlash against the minimalism popular in recent years. Instead of a clean, pared-down look, Scandinavians now like to mix it up and the new darker palette is accompanied by global influences from all over the world teamed with personal mementoes, antique furniture, plants and artworks.

GET THE LOOK

Daylight — or the lack of it — is something to bear in mind when choosing darker colours. Before you fall in love with a specific shade, buy a few sample pots and try colours on the wall or on a piece of lining paper. You will be surprised how much the appearance of a colour changes during the day as the daylight moves around a room.

White reflects light, while black absorbs it. The same applies to gloss levels in paint — a high-gloss finish reflects light, while a matte finish does not. When sombre colours are in vogue, it is important to know how to create a sense of light and space in a room even when the walls are dark. One trick is to paint the ceiling a lighter shade than the walls. It does not have to be white, but as the ceiling reflects a lot of the natural daylight, it will work well if the colour is slightly paler.

It is easy to produce a sleek, seamless effect with paint and there is a current trend to paint floors, walls and even the ceiling in the same hue. Rooms that are painted tone-on-tone can fool the eye and create the impression that a room is larger than it really is. Paint architectural features and woodwork the same colour as the walls and ceiling and allow furniture to bring contrast to the room.

BOLD ACCENTS

Another way to interpret Nordic colour is by focusing on bold accent colours. If Dark Eclectic draws inspiration from the colours of the natural landscape, this palette embraces the details that stand out and add character. Think of deep red lingonberries, blooming poppy fields or the vivid yellow leaves of the northern birch forests in early autumn. Very bright colours can be overpowering, but they feel less challenging when used as accents.

A colour accent is one used to bring emphasis and contrast to a scheme. Depending on how you combine colours, you can either accentuate or soften them. Some designers suggest that you pair up colours that sit close to each other on the colour wheel — so-called analogous colours, such as green and yellow or red and purple. Another way of creating contrast is to combine complementary colours, i.e. ones that sit directly opposite each other on the spectrum, such as green and red.

Colours of the same hue, or basic colour, can have a different chroma, saturation (intensity) and value (lightness/darkness of the colour). By taking into account these characteristics, you will be able to match contrasting colours that share the same nuances.

Scandinavian homes have traditionally been associated with a minimalist style – far from what we think of when we refer to colourful and bold. But flexible, creative and adventurous are also adjectives that can be used to describe the Scandis. Compared to other Europeans, young Swedes and Danes are the first to leave home, and tend to move several times in search of education, employment and travel. These circumstances have resulted in a sense of adventure and a playful, lighthearted approach to home decor.

GET THE LOOK

Choose one colour to use as a common thread through your space, then combine it with a complementary colour. Many paint companies have done the job for you and developed colour palettes where each hue is easy to match with another. Focus on one or two large areas or elements and match them with smaller details in the form of textiles or smaller objects.

Bold details can be balanced by neutral walls or teamed with an accent wall. Choose your colour with care, as it plays an important role in how the room will appear. To create a sense of space and light, use a lighter neutral on the walls and pick out the woodwork and architectural details in a darker hue. A long, narrow room will feel wider and squarer if the two shorter walls are painted in a darker shade.

Bold Accents is a look that's easy to achieve and will suit anyone who likes variety and change. Base your interior decisions on the room's size, light and layout, and experiment with colour on the floor, walls, furniture, fixtures and fittings. Even if your tastes tend to change, it's worth investing in classic designs in good materials and experimenting with wall colour when you feel the need for something new.

MAJESTIC PASTELS

For those who love colour but prefer lighter hues, pastels are a great alternative. Again, it's essential to take natural light and the aspect of a space into account when choosing colours. Light from the north or north-west will make colours look cooler and harder, and you may want to compensate by choosing a warm hue. Conversely, rooms with light from the south and east feel warm and bright. In Nordic homes, a pastel palette can intensify cold northern light in a beautiful way.

It is possible to draw parallels between the pastel colours that are appearing now and the hues that were popular in Scandinavia during the Gustavian era of the 1780s. The pastel shades so popular then are back — pearly grey, duck egg blue and salmon pink. Then, as now, clean lines were characteristic, but today it is a contemporary austerity that is desirable, rather than classic shapes. You can mix pastel-painted walls with natural materials such as stone and wood. Also consider teaming them with mirrors or shiny metals. Reflective surfaces create the illusion of a luminous interior by reflecting light and offering contrast to a muted background.

GET THE LOOK

Shades of pink and pale blue go well together. Pink is a warm colour and balances blue-grey hues effectively. It brings a sense of energy and peace, while blues are calming and refreshing. As modern pastels have black undertones, shades of grey will harmonize with them perfectly. If you are tempted by grey, bear in mind that it can be perceived as cold with a hint of mauve in north-facing rooms. To avoid a chilly effect, opt for a warm grey with yellow or red undertones.

In addition to colour, finish also plays an important role. When using modern pastels, opt for matte colours with low gloss levels to create a velvety, textured effect.

DARK
ECLECTIC

DARK AND HANDSOME

Five floors above Copenhagen's busy streets perches a penthouse apartment with wide-ranging views. Here, interior designer and store owner Michala Jessen has created her own universe, with personal treasures showcased against a dark, monochromatic backdrop. Michala has embraced the apartment's modernist architecture and its sleek lines offer an interesting counterpoint to a collection of handcrafted pieces, artworks and tactile textiles. Michala has followed her own style compass to create a home that combines urban glamour with eclectic charm.

ABOVE LEFT AND RIGHT Michala Jessen's apartment is filled with personal objects and pieces from her shop, Rue Verte. The spherical table lamp is by the Italian glass studio Gallotti & Radice. Michala's boyfriend, Danish artist Morten Angelo, created several of the artworks in her apartment; the painting in the kitchen is one of them.

OPPOSITE The dark colours in every room melt together in a harmonious way, while the finishes and materials add contrast. In the living room, the walls are painted a deep, dark green that verges on black. The ceiling is painted the same colour, but instead of a matte finish, Michala has used a high gloss to bounce light around the interior.

In the very heart of Copenhagen in elegant Frederiksstaden, just a stone's throw from the city's most historic sights, Michala and her son live in this considered, elegant apartment on the top floor of a 1950s block. The penthouse boasts a 120 sq.m./1291 sq.ft. wraparound terrace and sunlight floods in from the large windows. The apartment has the famous 18th-century Frederiks Kirke as a neighbour, and its stately Rococo architecture and patinated copper dome is reflected in the decor of the apartment, where dark, dull green-painted walls provide a backdrop for glittering steel, gleaming brass and plush textiles.

Michala opened her high-end interior design store Rue Verte in 1994. Located in a 250-year-old listed building nearby, it is decorated just like a private home. Many of the pieces in Michala's apartment can also be found in the store and it has a similar colour scheme. However, Rue Verte has a very different energy to the apartment, because of its original architectural mouldings and the building's quirky nooks and crannies.

Thanks to the success of her store, Michala has had a great deal of experience in helping people decorate their homes. Her philosophy is to first consider a home's location before deciding on the style of decor, and to embrace a property's original architecture instead of trying to work against or around it. Her own home is proof that Michala practises what she preaches. As this is a city-centre apartment surrounded by sweeping views of the urban skyline, she decided to give the space a cosmopolitan vibe with a sophisticated, sombre colour palette. The petrol green and dark grey hues give the modern architecture a sense of authority, and painting the ceilings the same colour as the walls gives the space a seamless feel. Finding the right shades was not easy — Michala tested 13 colours before she found exactly the right ones.

The building's modernist architecture is reflected in the open-plan kitchen, where the brushed stainless-steel surfaces are reminiscent of mid-20th-century tableware from Sweden and Denmark as well as aircraft galley kitchens. When Michala renovated the apartment a few years ago, she knocked out the wall between the kitchen and the living area to create an airier feel and a social connection between the two spaces.

A sense of timelessness is evident here. Michala explains that she has made decorative decisions based on her own taste rather than passing trends. To stay true to her individual sense of style, she tends to avoid reading interiors magazines and

OPPOSITE AND ABOVE
Behind the doors of a vintage wooden cabinet lies a treasure trove of tableware from all around the world. The handmade ceramics and lustrous metalware bring visual interest and a sense of history to the interior.

THIS PAGE In the open-plan living area, daylight bounces off the shiny metal and translucent glass surfaces. The glorious emerald-coloured velvet modular couch from Italian company Meridiani stands out against the subdued tones of deepest green and aubergine. To furnish the apartment, Michala chose to combine modern Danish craftsmanship with brands from southern Europe. The wire bar stool in the foreground is from Overgaard & Dyrman, while many of the light fittings were designed by Michala and her colleagues.

OPPOSITE Unlike the contemporary styling of the rest of the apartment, stepping into the bedroom feels like visiting a Venetian palace. The walls are painted in a mossy blue-green and a varied mix of fabrics with different textures creates contrast. Washed linen sheets, a knitted throw and lustrous velvet curtains meet delicate lace on the artwork above the bed, which is by photographer and visual artist Trine Søndergaard.

draws inspiration from her travels and from hotels and restaurants all over the world. She describes how, when she was choosing the materials for the kitchen, brass and copper were in vogue, but she opted for stainless steel instead – a material she loves, regardless of what is currently in fashion. This is the perfect illustration of her belief that if you create an interior that is rooted in your own personal taste, you won't tire of it.

The reflective surfaces, unusual lamps and gloss-painted ceilings in the living room all amplify the daylight, which brightens up the penthouse. Michala says she put a lot of time and effort into choosing lighting, partly because the decorative

light fittings create a dramatic effect against the monochrome walls, but also because good artificial lighting is a necessity in Denmark during the dark winter months.

Michala's apartment breathes sophisticated glamour. The atmosphere is part luxury hotel, part art gallery. Here and there, beloved objects demand our attention. Art, modern furniture and ethnic pieces from around the globe have been carefully chosen and curated by Michala. The colour palette may make a bold statement, but it is the eclectic mix of personal treasures that really makes her home stand out from the crowd.

ABOVE To the left of the window are narrow shelves that house decorative pieces, books and scented candles. Putting a traditional glass display cloche over scented candles not only looks attractive but also preserves the aromas and protects the candle from dust.

LEFT In the bedroom, as in the living room, Michala has chosen pieces of furniture that stand out against the dark backdrop. The rich yellow velvet armchair positioned in one corner of the room echoes golden accents elsewhere and glows in the sunlight that shines into the apartment all day long.

CALM AND COLLECTED

The home of Norway's brightest design exports and boutique owners,
Jannicke Kråkvik and Alessandro D'Orazio, could not be described as a typically
Scandinavian interior. The overall impression is of a dark, eclectic, almost Parisian
elegance, yet there is still something about the space that is identifiably
Scandinavian – it is calm, ordered and functional. What stands out the most
are the shadowy grey-blue walls, which bring a poetic serenity to the interior and
echo the waters of the Indre Oslofjord just outside their Oslo apartment.

OPPOSITE The kitchen units were handmade by Frama, a Danish design studio and frequent collaborator with the Kråkvik & D'Orazio creative studio. It was built as a mobile studio kitchen, but fits perfectly in this imposing room with its high ceilings and original stucco cornicing/crown moldings.

ABOVE LEFT AND RIGHT The couple collect Japanese pottery and these are a few of their favourite pieces. The kitchen cabinets were constructed from Douglas fir, stone and steel, and have a black countertop, sink and tap/faucet. Irregular wooden chopping boards add some character to the austere lines.

The couple have lived and worked together since 2003, and their creative studio, Kråkvik & D'Orazio, is celebrated for its projects both with Norwegian brands in Scandinavia and worldwide. The company undertakes interior design projects as well as commercial styling commissions. The couple have an experimental approach to colour and, thanks to a close collaboration with the Norwegian paint label Jotun and the company's creative director Lisbeth Larsen, Jannicke and Alessandro have learned a great deal about how colours interact and complement each other.

Their apartment is situated in a period property dating back to 1899. The main part of the interior consists of three beautifully proportioned rooms arranged *en enfilade* and all the original architectural features and ornamental mouldings are still intact.

LEFT The main living rooms overlook the street and are all painted a smoky grey-blue colour from Norwegian paint brand Jotun. The bedroom is at one end of the enfilade and the kitchen at the other, with the living room in between. Jannicke says they always have the doors open to keep the energy flowing through the space.

PAGE 42 The wooden floors of the apartment were treated with linseed oil to achieve a pale, creamy bone shade. On the wall behind the double door is the steel Eiffel lamp from Danish brand Frama.

PAGE 43 A textured brass folding screen seems to positively glow against the shadowy backdrop. The chair is by Harry Bertoia for Knoll and the lamp is an Akari Light Sculpture by lighting maestro Isamu Noguchi. The open doorway provides a glimpse into the hallway, where the walls have been left bare as a reminder of the apartment's history.

THIS PAGE Around the table stands a mix of vintage Thonet bentwood chairs and Chair One B by Konstantin Grcic for Magis. Coincidentally, the kitchen table is almost exactly the same colour as the walls. It came from their boutique, Kollekted By, but now fits in perfectly here. Jannicke says you cannot plan your home too closely – it's important to leave some space for happy accidents.

ABOVE LEFT Jannicke and Alessandro like to collect ceramics while on their travels. They are both passionate about Norwegian and Japanese crafts.

ABOVE RIGHT The couple use a lot of greenery in their styling work and when a project is finished they tend to bring any unwanted plants home with them. Their indoor garden started with one plant; now they have a small jungle. The wall art is by the photographer Sigve Asplund, a friend of the couple, and the plant artwork on the floor is by Danish sculptor Martin Erik Andersen.

OPPOSITE The sleek, minimal Modern Line sofa is from Danish brand Gubi, while the cork and black marble Sintra side table is by Frama and available from the couple's boutique, Kollekted By.

To demarcate between this area and the newly renovated study/office space and bathroom in the other part of the apartment, Jannicke and Alessandro painted the sections in very different colours. In the new bathroom and home office area, raw concrete floors are teamed with very light pink walls. In the enfilade rooms, which feature tall windows overlooking the street, the wooden floorboards were bleached to a pale buff hue and the doors, walls and architraves were painted a rich, stately grey-blue. Jannicke says that the smoky blue tone creates a calm, coherent atmosphere that ties everything together and works as a backdrop for their carefully chosen furnishings. With white walls, she says, the contrasts are sometimes too conspicuous.

Jannicke's advice is to bravely embrace colour. As the walls play a dominant role in any space, a coat of paint can have a transformative effect. Ringing the changes with paint is not expensive, and to keep costs down you can even do it yourself. Jannicke and Alessandro have a design philosophy that they adhere to both when it comes to professional projects and home — they always keep one wall bare in every room and prefer to pare down the contents rather than add to them. The result is that special treasures can enjoy the spotlight.

In the course of their job, Jannicke and Alessandro have access to a huge range of different furnishing and decorative products, and this has made them very discriminating when it comes to choosing items for their own home — objects are carefully considered

LEFT The chair is the Gaudi, designed by Vico Magistretti in 1970 for Italian brand Artemide. Its glossy grass green curves pop against the subdued grey wall. In every room, at least one wall remains bare — Jannicke says it's a good way to achieve a sense of balance and give space to the things you really love.

OPPOSITE The other part of the apartment has a very different feeling and a more modern vibe. Before the renovation, this office was a small kitchen, but Jannicke and Alessandro decided to move it to one of the larger rooms. The unusual wooden storage chest is the Sutoa from Frama.

before they cross the threshold. So what has made the grade? Some pieces were brought back from foreign flea markets, others were designed by Norwegian craftspeople and many items were handpicked from their own boutique, Kollekted By, which they opened in 2013 in Oslo's trendy Grünerløkka district. For obvious reasons, their store and home have many similarities.

The apartment appears carefully composed, with its dark walls, leafy plants, feature lighting, treasured pieces and contrasting textures creating a sense of calm completeness. But in reality, it seems that the interior came together without too much thought or forward planning. For a couple of the international design world's most celebrated stylists, Jannicke

and Alessandro have an unusually relaxed approach to their own home. They say there was not any specific concept, plan or source of inspiration behind the decor — their living space has just evolved naturally, one step at a time.

The couple purchased the apartment in the early 2000s and for many years lived with it just as it was. Two years ago, they felt the time was finally right for a complete renovation. But even once the wheels had been put in motion, the couple were in no hurry and the refurbishment proved to be a slow and steady process, taking about a year to accomplish. This was partly due to the lead time for the kitchen, which was made by Danish studio Frama. The minimalist, contemporary look of the kitchen cabinets, constructed from Douglas fir, stone and steel, provides an unexpected contrast to the apartment's stately architecture and ornate stucco ceiling mouldings.

Calmness and contrast are qualities that characterize Jannicke and Alessandro's relationship as much as their home. They met at a birthday party 15 years ago, moved in together and have never looked back. Alessandro's Italian roots and Jannicke's Norwegian heritage have come together to create a unique sense of style that is both Italian and Scandinavian, sophisticated and functional, masculine and feminine, eclectic and minimalistic. And perhaps it's because they haven't tried too hard that their apartment comes so close to perfection.

OPPOSITE The bed is dressed in minimalist fashion as the couple favour plain linen sheets in white and pale grey. The striking woven blanket placed on top was made by young Dutch textile designer Mae Engelgeer. It brings a note of colour and comfort to the space.

ABOVE RIGHT In the bedroom, Alessandro designed a whole wall of storage and left one small opening in the middle, which is now home to a stack of books and a vase designed by Norwegian ceramic artist Lillian Tørlen. The couple discovered her work at an exhibition where her ceramics had been attached to different surfaces in a room — the ceiling, corners and so on.

BELOW RIGHT The 90° Shelf Wall Light is by Frama and acts as both bedside light and handy shelf. Its simple, industrial styling is elevated by the rich glow of the brass, which looks particularly effective against the grey wall.

JEWELLED HUES

Behind the brick facade of a 1930s townhouse in Copenhagen lies a hidden gem. Goldsmith and jewellery designer Rebekka Notkin and her family live in this Art Deco-inspired home against a backdrop of Danish vintage finds, a fine glass collection and rich, jewel-coloured walls. The skills and aesthetics of Rebekka's profession of jewellery designer is reflected in the home's perfectly balanced spaces and the soul of the house whispers that everything here has a story. Rebekka's magical home is certainly one of a kind.

ABOVE LEFT The hand-painted cranes on the living room wall are one of the reasons Rebekka could never imagine moving from here. By De Gournay, they are painted in a special colourway on blue-grey dyed silk. The rattan armchair came from a store in Tisvilde in North Zealand. Together with the broad-leaf fig, this area feels like an exotic garden.

ABOVE RIGHT The turquoise pot with a surface pattern was, like everything in this home, chosen for its good looks. The little bowl on the lower level of the side table was designed by Bjørn Wiinblad, a Danish designer who had great success worldwide during the mid-20th century and has enjoyed a revival in recent years.

THIS PAGE The arresting artwork is by Rebekka's friend Asger Mortensen, while the white glass pieces on top of the 1930s trolley are part of Rebekka's collection of vintage opaline glass.

THIS PAGE AND OPPOSITE The kitchen successfully combines classical glamour and Scandinavian modernity. The pairing of yellow gold and red gemstones is a timeless motif in jewellery design. Here, the colour combination is recreated in the form of kitchen cabinets painted a deep, ruby red and subtle brass detailing. The windows are unencumbered by curtains or blinds, which allows light to flow in and highlight the simple aesthetic of the lamps, the brass details and the clean modern lines.

LEFT Rebekka and her husband have tried to preserve as many of the house's architectural details as possible. The original staircase and doors are still intact, while the old pine floor has been oiled in a dark hue to create a solid foundation for the rooms and complement the jewel-coloured walls.

PAGES 50 AND 51 The narrow hallway leads to an entrance room decorated with prints and art by Danish artists Tal R and Evren Tekinoktay from the Schäfer Grafisk Værksted. The dull blue walls provide the perfect backdrop for the distinctive artworks, glass sculptures and brass decorations.

Sometimes it's not until you step into a colourful interior that you realize how much you miss joyful, vibrant colours in a world of white, minimalist spaces. Colour and pattern add character, spark positive energy and kick-start creativity. That's exactly what happens when you enter Danish jewellery designer Rebekka Notkin's home. Every vase, painting and candleholder in here tells a special story and the house has the atmosphere of a fantasy universe from a childhood dream.

Rebekka's brick townhouse dates from the 1930s and is located in Frederiksberg, a fashionable, leafy neighbourhood in the Danish capital. The house is part of a historic terrace designed by Thorkild Henningsen, a famous Danish architect active during the transition from Neoclassicism to functionalism in the early 1900s. The dignified brick facade conceals a well-preserved home with many original features and a unique atmosphere.

The house was originally built for an artist, something revealed by the huge studio window upstairs. And, in a case of history repeating itself, almost 100 years later goldsmith and jewellery designer Rebekka Notkin and her family live here. Rebekka believes there is a special atmosphere in the house and she and her husband have tried to

LEFT AND RIGHT

The dusky blue walls of the living room provide a subdued backdrop for furniture, art and decorative details. Above the sofa hangs a poetic artwork by Astrid Kruse Jensen, named 'Within the Landscape'. The Spanish Chairs are a Danish design classic, originally designed by Børge Mogensen in 1958, and the circular table decorated with birds by Bjørn Wiinblad dates back to the 1960s and is a treasured possession. Rebekka found it while on vacation in Hamburg and took a detour to buy the table on her way home.

preserve it by making sensitive renovations and retaining as many architectural features as possible. The stairways and doors are all original, while the old pine floors have been oiled to a dark brown hue to create a solid base for the rooms and highlight the coloured walls.

The house is an endless source of inspiration for Rebekka. An ornamental detail on the brick facade or an architectural feature might provide the idea for a new piece of jewellery, and at the same time some of the colour combinations here are drawn from her designs. In the kitchen, for example, a gold-painted wall is combined with glinting brass fixtures and glossy, deep ruby red cabinets.

Rebekka opened her first boutique and atelier in Copenhagen in 1997 after finishing her goldsmith training. Her passionate approach to craftsmanship, and especially metalworking, was inherited from her father, who was a goldsmith by profession, and her grandfather, who was a dental technician. Rebekka inherited their tools and still uses them today. Nowadays, she has two entrancing boutiques, one on fashionable Bredgade in Copenhagen and the other in Hamburg, where she sells her sought-after pieces – all individually designed and inspired by history, myth and fantasy.

It is possible to draw parallels between Rebekka's designs and the decoration of her home. Both are strongly inspired by the Art Deco era, with its eclectic feminine mix of patterns,

LEFT AND ABOVE In the bedroom, Rebekka chose a dramatic crimson for the walls. The generous size of the room and the daylight that floods in from a skylight balance out the bold shade. The mood is calm and cosy thanks to the simple furnishings, and the bed is the focal point. Delicate floral patterns, a feminine still life with perfumes and the fresh, flamingo pink walls give the room a romantic yet avant-garde vibe.

materials, textures and colours. The clear hues of petrol blue, rich red and dusty green are a perfect backdrop for her elegant still lifes. Most of the objects are chosen for their beauty rather than their functionality. Rebekka explains that she is drawn to the Art Deco movement because of its decadence and spirit of optimism. It was also the first time that many female artists gained recognition and were able to shape their own style of expression.

Rebekka's own creative streak has been evident for as long as she can remember. She was the kind of child who spent a lot of time alone in her bedroom, decorating the walls of her dolls' house with wallpaper or creating elaborate narratives about other worlds. In her adult life, she tries to maintain that spirit of imagination, along with a sense of restrained elegance.

Her house is a short cycle ride from work and school, but the great location is not the only reason that Rebekka cannot imagine moving. In the living room, one wall is decorated with an exquisite hand-painted silk wallpaper depicting a group of cranes. 'It would be awful to abandon them,' she says.

As you walk around Rebekka's house, it wouldn't be a surprise to stumble across a Narnia-like alternative universe at the back of a wardrobe, or a tiny walnut-shell cradle on a windowsill. The house is full of quirky treasures found at auctions and flea markets. Rebekka says that when her children's friends come over to play they say that the house is special. The truth is you don't have to be a child to find it alluring — this elegant wonderland makes everyone believe in fairy tales again.

THIS PAGE Rebekka is drawn to naturalistic patterns, shapes and colours. There are plants and flowers throughout her home, not least in the bedroom where the sheets and coverlet feature soft florals, green leaves and waving palm trees.

A MODERN CLASSIC

Behind a sober, classical facade in Copenhagen's redeveloped Islands Brygge district lies interior designer Anders Krakau's handsome apartment. This sophisticated space boasts graceful proportions and original period features teamed with sleek modern furnishings. When it came to choosing a colour scheme, Anders drew his inspiration from the Nordic autumn, opting for a subtle palette of warm, dark hues. Despite the sombre tones of the decor, his apartment is still remarkably light and open in feel.

As with many cities, Copenhagen has an old industrial district that within just a few decades has been transformed from an undesirable and dilapidated spot to a fashionable, sought-after neighbourhood. Islands Brygge is a harbourfront area that was established through a programme of land reclamation that began in the 1880s. Its name translates roughly to Iceland Wharf, and it was from here that ships sailed to and from Iceland, which was at that time a Danish colony. During the first half of the 20th century, Islands Brygge was heavily industrialized, but during the second half of the century the industries based here entered a long decline and the district became derelict.

OPPOSITE When Anders moved into the apartment, the kitchen was a rather antiseptic white space. To give it more character and bring it into line with the rest of the apartment, Anders painted the cabinets in a dark greenish black and replaced the handles with burnished brass knobs that he designed himself.

ABOVE LEFT To achieve a coordinated and harmonious look throughout the apartment,

Anders opted for a palette of dark, moody shades that share the same tonal values.

ABOVE CENTRE On a brass table top is a cluster of ceramic bowls and a vintage wooden bowl from Indonesia.

ABOVE RIGHT In the living room, the grey-brown linen-covered sofa is from French brand La Fibule and perfectly matches the warm grey walls.

However, in the past 20 years the area has undergone a massive programme of redevelopment and it is now one of the city's trendiest and most popular neighbourhoods. Islands Brygge is characterized by a mixture of old buildings and new developments, and many of the original structures have now been converted into sought-after residential units. A couple of years ago, designer Anders Krakau moved into this apartment, which is located in a Nordic Classicist building dating back to 1920.

Anders knew that he wanted to give his new home a dark and moody look and, in search of an array of dark tones that would work well together, he looked at colour schemes based on those seen in nature. Scandinavians have a deep love of and sense of connection with the natural world around them, as

ABOVE In the kitchen, the bowls, plates and cups on the countertop come from Anders' own brand, Arrondissement Copenhagen. The ceramics are made of natural brown clay moulded by hand and their dark lustre is due to smoke firing at a certain temperature.

OPPOSITE Circular dining tables usually result in convivial conversations. This one was designed by Anders himself and is made from concrete and iron. The pendant light is the burnished brass and blown glass Bolle by Gallotti & Radice. Anders' elegant dining chairs are upholstered in a beautiful velvet fabric and, like many of the other furnishings in the apartment, come from Rue Verte, the boutique that he co-owns.

summed up by the Norwegian word *friluftsliv*, which describes an ancient Nordic appreciation of and closeness to nature. With its fallen leaves, shorter days and misty mornings, autumn is Anders' favourite season and so he decided to take it as his inspiration for the decor of the apartment. He chose a limited palette of rich, mellow grey-browns and darkest forest green in a chalky, flat finish from British paint brand Zoffany.

To prevent the interior from becoming too dark and sombre, Anders was careful to make sure there was enough contrast to enliven the spaces. The woodwork, architraves and ceilings are painted a bright, crisp white throughout and bring definition to the well-proportioned rooms. Anders has incorporated reflective surfaces such as glass and dull metal to bounce natural light around the rooms, while antique furnishings in dark polished wood contribute a rich, subtle glow of their own. The white details frame the rooms to perfection and stand out against the dark walls, while the light oak floors were treated with a brown wax oil to create a dark, matte finish that looks as if it has developed over the years.

Anders co-owns renowned Copenhagen concept store Rue Verte with Michala Jessen (see her home on pages 30—37) and they make several trips each year to the major design fairs in Paris, Milan and London to source new stock. As can be seen in the store, unlike the traditional Scandinavian style, with its natural materials, austere lines and organic shapes,

OPPOSITE The photograph hanging above the sofa is by Anders' friend Josephine Alberthe and was taken in the Kongens Have (King's Garden) park in central Copenhagen. The Eclipse chandelier from British brand Ochre is made from dark horn and is one of Anders' favourite pieces.

BELOW LEFT The elegant dark wood and rattan rocking chair is an heirloom handed down from Anders' girlfriend's grandparents. A pile of coffee-table books doubles as a side table in this tranquil reading corner.

BELOW RIGHT A generously stocked drinks trolley or bar harks back to a more elegant time and makes pre-dinner drinks something of an occasion. Anders' home bar is also a beautiful addition to the decor, with its crystal decanters, cut glass and vintage cocktail shaker.

Anders is drawn to a more luxurious look, with tactile velvet curtains and upholstery and polished dark wood furniture – a style that is more common in France and Italy. However, the harbourfront location of the apartment is also referenced in the décor – industrial-luxe materials including raw linen, leather and unpolished iron all put in an appearance and contrast beautifully with the calm, classical vibe.

Many of the handsome pieces in the apartment were sourced by Anders on his travels, but quite often he has a vision of a particular item or object that proves impossible to find. His solution? To design it himself, of course. In 2015, together with Therese Torgersen, Anders established Arrondissement Copenhagen, a Danish company that creates timeless, high-quality, custom-made furniture, and their designs can be found throughout the apartment.

Good craftsmanship is at the heart of the Arrondissement concept and the materials are chosen with great care and attention to detail. Ceramic bowls and plates are handmade from natural brown clay, fired in a wood-burning kiln and smoked at a high temperature to create a dense lustre. Tables are crafted from tarnished iron and hand-finished leather, while the knobs on Anders' kitchen cabinets were specially made of burnished brass that will slowly develop a rich patina. All the designs have longevity in mind and Arrondissement pieces will only grow more beautiful with the passage of time.

OPPOSITE The apartment is situated in a building built in the Nordic Classicism style of the 1920s. The large windows allow natural daylight to flood into the interior and to accentuate the graceful architectural features. Anders painted all the ceilings and the woodwork a clean, crisp white to provide definition and frame the moody hues that cover the walls. When the daylight fades away, the Eclipse chandelier casts a rich, mellow light and provides the room with a glamorous focal point.

ABOVE AND BELOW RIGHT Every room in the apartment is painted in a carefully chosen hue from English brand Zoffany, renowned for the great depth of colour of their paints. The furnishings are minimal, but every piece tells a story. Next to an old Chinese table stands a leather chair that Anders inherited from his grandfather (above right), while beside this small velvet-covered ottoman is a Circle side table from Anders' company Arrondissment Copenhagen (below right).

LEFT In the bedroom, a wooden dressing table enjoys pride of place. It was inherited from Anders' girfriend's grandparents and is adorned with a brass lamp, jewellery display and a scented candle that add a glamorous touch. In this room, Anders retained the original dado rail/chair rail and painted the wall beneath it white to provide contrast with the dark floor.

OPPOSITE Anders designed a bespoke storage unit to hold clothes and accessories in the bedroom. The doors have bevelled panels that give the cabinets the same traditional character as the architectural features in the rest of the apartment. The bed is dressed in soft linens in restful hues of dark brown and midnight blue. The wall lamp in brass from Restart Milano provides light to read by.

In Anders' bedroom, he designed a practical custom-built fitted wardrobe/closet that surrounds the bed and offers ample storage space. It was especially designed to match the apartment's architectural features and the bevelled panels on the doors give the unit a traditional character that ties in with the room's original dado rail/chair rail and window frames. The cabinetry has been painted the same soft, sludgy khaki hue as the rest of the room so that it appears to just blend into the walls.

During the last hundred years, Islands Brygge has changed from a gritty working-class waterfront area with many small factories and workers' housing into a fashionable residential quarter. The imaginative redevelopment has brought new life and new inhabitants into the area, and the recently established shops, restaurants, harbour park, open-air swimming pool and the varied architecture positioned right by the water's edge make this neighbourhood an attractive place to live.

BOLD
ACCENTS

BRINGING COLOUR TO LIFE

With a passion for colour, a working life that has honed his sense for shades and hues and a willingness to experiment, it comes as no surprise that white is out of the picture in designer Daniel Heckscher's apartment. The 1980s building's apricot facade, along with his daughter's love of pink, influenced his choice of wall colour, while the complementary blue on the floor is a reference to the family's former house in the Stockholm archipelago. This is a home that pushes the boundaries and celebrates the sheer sensual pleasure of vibrant colour.

ABOVE LEFT The herringbone hall floor is the only white detail in the apartment. The pattern is formed by narrow rectangular tiles and meets a pink standard tile that is set on the diagonal on the walls. The coloured grouting between the tiles is a detail that creates contrast and provides an intriguing visual effect.

ABOVE RIGHT The same type of standard square tile appears in the kitchen, but in a light green hue. Daniel knocked through part of the wall between the kitchen and living room when he bought the apartment. The opening creates an airy space and the marble-topped bar is the family's favourite place to eat breakfast in the mornings.

THIS PAGE The salmon pink walls are in tune with the pastel pink facade of the block, which can be seen from the apartment's balcony. The moulding that covers the bottom part of the wall is painted the same blue as the floors, and to create a seamless effect, the ceiling is a light grey-blue hue.

ABOVE LEFT The modernist mouldings with diagonal stripes give character to the walls in the living room. The diagonal motif is repeated in the herringbone tile on the hallway floor. When Daniel bought the apartment, it was essentially a white box – the ideal opportunity for a designer to try out new, playful ideas.

ABOVE RIGHT The home is filled with items that have special meaning for Daniel. The small green marble table by Nick Ross was found at the Örnsbergsauktionen, an artist-run auction of studio-produced design and craft objects by Swedish and international designers held once a year, just outside of Stockholm.

A 30-minute drive from central Stockholm, in one of the archipelago's many bays, stands an apartment block dating back to 1988. The building itself, boasting a pastel apricot facade that stands out among the pines of the neighbourhood, is fairly typical of 1980s architecture, but a spectacular surprise awaits inside.

This is the home of interior architect Daniel Heckscher and his two children, Otis and India. The rich, saturated colours that dominate the space might seem daring at first sight, but the bold shades here make perfect sense when you learn that Daniel is part of Swedish design studio Note, which has gained a reputation worldwide for projects with adventurous palettes.

Daniel describes himself as drawn to design that affects people and evokes some sort of emotional response or leaves a lasting impression. It might be hard to pinpoint exactly what that impression is, or difficult to feel it right away, but you will take something with you when you leave. For him, this compact apartment offered somewhere to experiment in a playful way.

The warm orange-pink hue in the living area makes reference to the exterior of the apartment building (which is visible from the living room and kitchen area), and it was also chosen by Daniel's daughter India. He asked both children which colours they would like to have in their new home and India opted for pink, while son Otis wanted gold and black. To avoid too much

of a mismatch, Daniel plumped for a soothing pink palette and gave his son a new bicycle helmet in his favourite colours instead.

The children were at the forefront of Daniel's mind when it came to decorating the apartment. The kitchen tiles and the saturated blue of the flooring and wall mouldings are reminiscent of their previous home, where the family lived before Daniel's divorce. He explains that it felt right to use a colour scheme that the children were already familiar with. The colours in the living area set the tone for the rest of the apartment; deep blue-green and powdery pink mingle with bright yellow accents and a playful mix of patterns and textures. The ceramic herringbone tiles in the hallway are the only touch of white in the interior.

Daniel was partly educated abroad. Despite a background in economics, he was attracted to a more creative profession and was close to 30 when he began studying interior and spatial design, first in Milan and then at the prestigious Konstfack (University of Arts, Crafts and Design) in Stockholm. Although his career change came relatively late in life, strong colour and form have always fascinated him, and his love of colour was only enhanced by time spent abroad.

Daniel's theory is that many people opt for white or neutral interiors because they are nervous about choosing the 'right' colour and are frightened of making a mistake. However, life is not colourless. Even on the greyest winter day in Sweden, a thousand different shades can be seen just outside the window. He points out that few people would choose white or grey as their favourite colour and therefore it's strange that so many of us choose to decorate our homes in this way.

To anyone used to images of pared-back or monochrome Scandinavian interiors and stark white walls, the dramatic colour choices in this home might not seem to be traditionally Nordic.

OPPOSITE Daniel emphasizes that many of the materials used in his home were far from expensive, but they were chosen with care. The coloured tiles and grouting make all the difference in the kitchen, while the lamp from Established & Sons and the stools from Cappellini offer colourful contrasting accents.

ABOVE The oil painting is by Daniel's grandfather, who worked in a bank for his whole life but was also a talented artist. On the wall behind hangs a print by Mari Helen Wahlberg, a classmate of Daniel's from Konstfack. The sleek chair is from Muuto and the candlesticks are from Normann Copenhagen and Iittala.

On the other hand, when it comes to design and decoration, this apartment is identifiably Scandinavian in the sense that it manages to be uncluttered and functional yet still warm and welcoming. The tiled hall floor can be mopped quickly and easily after muddy mountain bikes and slushy shoes have made their mark. Daniel has also paid a great deal of attention to the lighting, which has to work well because the family spend most of the time in their apartment when it is dark outside. Nordic homes need effective lighting to cater for the long winters, while summer days tend to be spent out of doors.

Even though the family love their home and are very happy here, Daniel admits that part of him longs to get his teeth into an exciting new project. But as he wants to remain in the same area, it's a bit of a Catch-22. Moreover, it would be difficult to introduce any new colours into the apartment, as everything is so harmoniously matched. One thing is for sure, the current colour palette is perfect — and leaves no one untouched.

ABOVE AND OPPOSITE Instead of a traditional headboard, Daniel attached a framework of diagonal strips to the wall behind the bed to create a decorative panelled effect. The tranquil blue-green tone is a restful shade for a bedroom and recurs in the adjacent kids' room and in the hall. As those spaces have less natural daylight, Daniel used a slightly lighter shade of paint there, but clever lighting makes the difference in colour almost imperceptible. The rule of thumb is that the closer to a light source you are, the darker you can afford to go.

SECOND TIME AROUND

A spacious and serene villa in the peaceful Copenhagen suburb of Gentofte is home to Danish art collector and gallerist Sara Lysgaard. Once decorated in a fashionably pale and pared-down Scandinavian palette, her recently redecorated home boldly embraces colour and pattern. A break-up a few years ago proved a turning point both personally and stylistically, and gave Sara the opportunity to develop her own vision. The result is a glamorous yet playful interior full of art and colour that gives her energy and inspiration.

ABOVE LEFT Sara Lysgaard grew up surrounded by art – a legacy that has continued into her adult life. In a corner of her living room hangs a piece by British artist David Shrigley alongside a small Bubbly lamp by Rosie Li, a puddle sculpture on the floor by art group AKassen and a playful neon piece by Gun Gordillo.

ABOVE RIGHT Sara turned to Jannik Martensen-Larsen, owner of Copenhagen's renowned Tapet-Café, for help in finding the right colour palette, rugs and textiles for her home. It took the two of them just 30 minutes to make their decisions. Sara chose Farrow & Ball paint throughout and the petrol blue-grey in the living room is Inchyra Blue.

PAGE 81 The flooring throughout the house was treated with white hard wax to achieve a light, semi-matte finish. It's a perfect match for the grey Wishbone or Y-chairs from Hans J Wegner that surround a marble-topped dining table by another iconic Danish designer, Poul Kjærholm. The geometric Lina pendant light in brass hanging above the table is by the Chinese-born American designer Rosie Li and was inspired by 1960s Italian lighting. The red box made from salvaged materials just seen on the floor behind the table is by Brooklyn-based artist Graham Collins.

Once a popular summer retreat for Copenhagen's wealthy bourgeoisie, Gentofte is now a leafy, pleasant suburb located just ten minutes away from the city centre. The house where Sara lives was originally a large family home complete with gardens and stables, but it has been converted into separate units that now house six families. Her portion of the house is split over two floors and has its own lovely garden.

Sara moved in seven years ago, along with her boyfriend. Their newly renovated house was a clean white shell with white walls, white curtains and bleached wooden floors. Simple and stylish, the pared-down, typically Scandinavian interior suited the couple perfectly at the time. But times change, and when Sara's relationship came to an end, she decided that she wanted to remain in the house but to make a fresh start and create a new home to suit her new life.

Sara began the process by putting all of her furniture, art and other possessions into storage, leaving her with a blank canvas. Realizing that she had a new appetite for bold colour, she turned to Jannik Martensen-Larsen — a friend who also happens to be the owner of celebrated Danish design company Tapet-Café, which was founded in 1974 and is located in an old house close by in Gentofte. Sara asked Jannik to realize her vision

ABOVE AND OPPOSITE Sara chooses art by instinct and she has the same philosophy when it comes to selecting furniture. In the living room, the yellow velvet chaise longue from Danish company Eilersen is accompanied by the Diamond table from FOS and green and blue Lens tables with resin tops by British designers McCollin Bryan. The Moroccan rug is vintage, from Copenhagen store The Apartment. Daylight is reflected in the mirror piece by Henry Krokatsis and Adonis artwork by Elmgreen & Dragset.

PAGE 84 The living room has all the ingredients that are important for a warm and welcoming home: plants, textiles, light and colour. The elegant lines of the Gubi sofa are softened by cushions from Tapet-Café and the artwork is by Tom Humphreys.

PAGE 85 The French doors are screened by simple white curtains. The artwork is by David Shrigley and the floral rug is Fleurelle by Helene Blanche, a famous Danish textile designer and Jannik's wife.

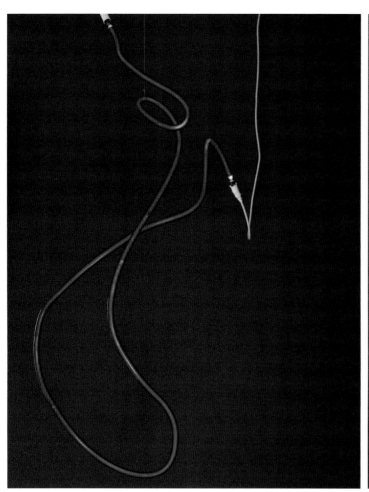

ABOVE LEFT The sculptural blue neon squiggle is by the Swedish-Danish artist Gun Gordillo. She has been working with light for more than 25 years, making the pieces herself in her studio. Well known in the Scandinavian art world, she is now popular on the international stage as well.

ABOVE RIGHT Paint-splattered coffee mugs from the LA-based ceramic artist Peter Shire reflect the changes in Sara's home over the past few years — from plain white to a vibrant spectrum of colour.

OPPOSITE A wooden staircase leads upstairs. The walls are Light Blue from Farrow & Ball and in the stairwell hangs an installation with soccer balls by Colombian artist Dario Escobar. The two paintings hung adjacent to each other in the corner are by New York-based artist Landon Metz. The timeless kitchen boasts glossy, white cabinets and had just been installed by the previous owner when Sara moved in, almost seven years ago.

of a home filled with timeless yet bold colours and richly patterned textiles in matching hues. With Jannik's encouragement and collaboration, Sara was able to commit to her vision of a colourful home.

The results are breathtaking. A palette of petrol blue, peppermint, powder pink, grass green and citrus yellow is combined with attention-grabbing artworks, patterned rugs and eclectic furnishings. Sara does not miss her all-white interior, saying that, while it suited her at the time, in retrospect it was bland and didn't make enough of a statement. Her attitude towards colour has undergone a complete change during the past few years, and Sara describes herself as something of a colour addict now, automatically opting for rich, vibrant shades when it comes to clothing, furniture and art. She explains that the transformation of her home has allowed her to be true to herself and her own personal tastes.

Sara grew up in a home that was filled with art. At the tender age of 18, she asked her father to withdraw all the funds from her childhood savings account so that she could buy her first piece. Today, as well as an art collector, Sara is

EXISTENCE
WHAT DOES
IT MATTER
I EXIST
ON THE BEST
TERMS
I CAN
THE PAST IS NOW PART OF MY
FUTURE
TH PRESENT
IS WELL OUT OF

OPPOSITE AND BELOW Sara's bedroom is painted in Setting Plaster by Farrow & Ball – a soft, restful pink. The large artwork is by Michael Bevilacqua and the cerise lamp is vintage, as is the vibrant Moroccan rug on the floor. The pink artwork hanging above a low stool is by Danish artist Troels Sandegaard (below), while the two works on the floor are by Morten Ernlund Jørgensen.

RIGHT Sara describes her bedroom as a beautiful, soft bubble. Previously the walls were white, but thanks to the high ceiling and the large windows, Sara says the room was almost too dazzlingly bright. The eyes artwork to the left of the bed is by Sven Dalsgaard.

owner of a holding company that makes various investments, and, until recently, was a partner in a gallery in Mallorca. As part of her job, Sara travels to art fairs around the world and cities such as Venice, New York and Paris, among others, and says she feels privileged to be able to visit some of the world's most beautiful cities on a regular basis. However, despite the globe trotting to glamorous destinations, Sara says that landing at Copenhagen airport is her favourite feeling. During her travels she leads a busy and sociable existence, so for her home is a place to retreat, rest and recharge the batteries.

Sara's art collection is eclectic and diverse, encompassing paintings, photographs, drawings, sculptures and more. Each and every piece has a story behind it and was chosen with thought, love and care. When it comes to buying, Sara looks for works that she has an immediate connection with and which speak to her in some way. It used to be believed that white walls provided the best backdrop for contemporary art, but in recent years they have started to look slightly outdated and most galleries have embraced softer hues. The strong, saturated wall colours in Sara's home perfectly showcase her collection, although Sara declares

LEFT Upstairs is a home office-cum-guest room. The slanted ceiling was painted in Farrow & Ball's Stone Blue and the walls in contrasting Calke Green for a fresh, playful effect. The elegantly minimal table lamp on the desk is the Get Set by Michael Anastassiades and the wall is hung with colourful pieces by several different artists.

OPPOSITE The white sofa from Meridiani doubles up as a bed for overnight guests. The green walls set off the vibrant orange artwork by French artist Philippe Parreno that hangs behind the sofa and the large-scale abstract painting by Clare Woods with its warm orange and brown tones. The rug is by Richard Colman for Danish brand Hay.

that neither the colour palette nor the furnishings were deliberately chosen to match the art. Friends and acquaintances have sometimes sought her advice on buying artworks to match a decorative scheme, but Sara maintains that art should be chosen because it sparks an emotional connection, not purely to match an interior decorator's mood board.

When she talks about her home, Sarah compares it to life in general: always changing, constantly evolving. The original decor — white, cool and pared-down — has developed into something colourful, confident and bold, and for the first time in a long while, Sara feels that her surroundings are completely in tune with her personality.

THIS PAGE Isabelle's apartment is located in Stockholm's bohemian SoFo district. The family's previous home was in the same neighbourhood and they only moved a few blocks to their new home. The apartment is a maisonette/duplex and the kids have their own space downstairs, while the living areas occupy the top floor.

DREAMING IN COLOUR

In the heart of Stockholm, interior designer, blogger and TV personality Isabelle McAllister has created a family home that's full of fun, distinctive designs and brave colour choices. It's a warm, convivial space furnished with flea-market bargains, quirky antiques and upcycled pieces, and the relaxed vibe signals that the inhabitants don't take themselves too seriously. Environmental awareness, untrammelled creativity and a passion for colour and pattern have all made their mark on Isabelle's cosy loft apartment.

ABOVE LEFT Concrete tiles by Scandinavian design trio Claesson Koivisto Rune for Marrakech Design cover the wall behind the hob/stovetop. The emerald green works well against the plaster pink walls and granite countertop, and the graphic detailing and asymmetrical arrangement make a bold design statement.

ABOVE RIGHT Isabelle chose an eco-friendly kitchen from Finnish company Puustelli Miinus. The materials and manufacturing process are non-toxic and all the parts can be reused or recycled. As a result, its carbon footprint is about 50 per cent less than a standard kitchen. The kitchen counter is extra deep to provide additional work space.

THIS PAGE Isabelle adores colour but says that finding the right combinations can sometimes be a challenge. The wall behind the wall tiles was originally mint green and the kitchen cabinets were a mid-blue. She thinks the current scheme of dusty pink walls and dark green cabinets suits the space much better. The bench in the foreground is a vintage Indian piece, the leaf wall lamp was found in Belgium and the wall-mounted pineapple sconce came from a market in Berlin.

OPPOSITE The powdery pink colour of the walls matches Isabelle's wedding dress, partly concealed by an oil painting to the right of the chimneybreast. In Isabelle's opinion, saturated pastels are a better base for a room than white – they add warmth and subtlety and don't get dirty and dingy. Just blending white paint with a few drops of pigment will result in more interesting walls.

BELOW LEFT AND RIGHT The apartment is filled with unique pieces and quirky details. The vintage Öglan cafe chairs from Ikea and the bubblegum pink table (seen opposite) were used in a job Isabelle did where children were allowed to paint an apartment that was for sale. A closer look at the chairs reveals that they are beautifully sprinkled with drops of cerise and orange paint.

As soon as you enter Isabelle McAllister's apartment, it is obvious that she is not afraid of colour. A plaster pink sitting room, forest green bedroom and a bathroom tiled in peppermint green are not unusual by Isabelle's standards. She is known as a colour advocate and uses television appearances, magazine articles and her blog to encourage her fellow Swedes to embrace colour and creativity. Paint and colour make Isabelle happy and she believes that it is difficult to design a cosy, beautiful home only using white — in her opinion, monochromatic interiors may be photogenic, but they are very hard to live in. Isabelle's theory is that the minimalist white homes we see all over social media are like pop songs – we listen to them on the radio and eventually we start to sing along, but is it because we actually like the music, or because we've heard it so many times that the tune has taken root in our brains? As for the old decorating rule that white is the only colour to use if you want to make a room appear lighter, she points out that we no longer live in the 17th century — effective lighting is available at the flick of a switch.

Isabelle's aesthetic is one of cheerful imperfection. Her bold tastes and resourceful attitude were instilled in her during her childhood, as both her parents worked with colour and design. Her mother is originally from Belgium and when Isabelle was a teenager the family moved there. She learned Flemish and began a course at art school, only to drop out and start designing lamps and styling homes instead. Her father, a scrap dealer and salvage merchant, still helps out with many of her projects and has a solution for every problem.

Isabelle's apartment is divided over two floors and the communal areas occupy the attic space. The open-plan living room-cum-kitchen has slanting ceilings, wooden beams and a huge fireplace taking up most of one wall, which posed something of a challenge when they first moved in. To begin with, Isabelle painted the kitchen cabinets sea blue and the walls of the kitchen area mint green, but after a while she reconsidered and repainted the walls a muted pink and the cabinets dark grey-brown. She says she often defaults to dusty pastels — they are neutral, soft and timeless, and combine happily with many other colours.

Isabelle didn't start with a grand plan or vision for the apartment. Instead, she likes to make a start decorating and see where she ends up. Her home is somewhere that allows her to experiment and try new things – when inspiration strikes, she unearths an old tin of paint from her cache and her husband comes home that night to discover that the furniture or walls have changed colour. For example, Isabelle recently repainted the bedroom a soft, luxurious dark green shade. She hasn't changed anything else in the room, but both she and her husband have noticed that now they use the room much more, going in there to read or relax.

Most of the items in Isabelle's apartment were discovered in flea markets and antiques shops, both

OPPOSITE Against the gallery wall stands a workbench that was previously used for carpentry work in the family's country house in Sweden's Dalarna province. The pink armchair was bought in Paris by Isabelle's mother many years ago and was reupholstered by Isabelle's father. Her parents are creatives who have worked with colour and design all their lives.

ABOVE A string of lights playfully delineates the slope of the roof. The old storage cabinet, which is on wheels, looks as if it might have had a previous life in a hospital or dental practice. Isabelle found it in a flea market.

OPPOSITE AND PAGE 102
The bedroom was recently repainted after a family holiday to Milan, where Isabelle was inspired by the decor of the hotel they stayed in. Isabelle is a dab hand at crafting and upcycling – she made the ochre cushions herself from old bath towels.

ABOVE LEFT In the bedroom, ornate vintage lamps featuring lustrous gold-coloured leaves stand out beautifully against the deep, dark green walls. Since the room was repainted, Isabelle finds it a much more welcoming and relaxing space.

ABOVE RIGHT The apartment has numerous charming yet awkward nooks and crannies. Isabelle had some fun with paint tester pots in this little niche in a corner of the bedroom. The ceiling is the same pink as the living room, while a small area of floor is painted a vibrant mustard yellow.

PAGE 103 The mint green and grey bathroom was newly renovated when the family moved in and Isabelle thought it would be very wasteful to tear everything out and start again. Instead, she is thinking about a few small changes to make the space truly her own.

at home and abroad. Upcycling is her speciality subject and she says a lick of paint or a length of fabric gives most items a new lease of life. Hunting for treasure at flea markets is one of her favourite activities. The most important thing for Isabelle is falling in love with an object. She is not interested in status symbols or iconic designer pieces and values character, comfort and personality in a home over impersonal perfection.

This is a friendly, easy-going space where everyone feels at home. Isabelle has allowed her kids free rein in their own rooms — her son has covered his walls with posters of footballers/soccer players and Isabelle was a little surprised when her pre-teen daughter wanted to paint her bedroom walls white. But then her daughter also recently suggested that they could transform a pair of her trousers into cool, bespangled shorts to wear to a party — so the creativity, recycling gene and desire to go one's own way seems to have been transmitted to the next generation too.

MAJESTIC
PASTELS

EMBRACING HISTORY

In this majestic residence in the affluent Östermalm district of central Stockholm, three perfectly preserved traditional ceramic-tiled stoves dating back to the 19th century provided the inspiration for a colour scheme that encompasses every aspect of the decor. Note Design Studio was tasked with adapting the period interior to make it suitable for modern family life. Their solution was to use a palette of warm pastel hues and to introduce a variety of interesting textures and patterns to provide further visual interest.

On the fourth floor of an unremarkable building in a quiet corner of Östermalm is an entirely remarkable modern family home. The rooms are lofty and imposing, and their stately period features are decorated in an unexpected palette of creamy pastel tones. The colour scheme manages to be distinctive without being overly dramatic or attention seeking — the main living rooms are bathed in a gentle, welcoming wash of colour that gives the impression that the sun is shining in through the tall windows all year round. As you wander from room to room, the subtlety of the scheme becomes apparent. Delicate hues of buttery yellow, mossy green, apricot and pale grey wash over the walls and

ABOVE LEFT AND RIGHT In the kitchen of this astonishing apartment the buttercup yellow walls give everything a warm, sun-kissed glow. Light wood furniture harmonizes perfectly with wall cupboards painted a saturated golden shade.

ABOVE CENTRE The kitchen island is made from polished terrazzo. This lively material is flecked with yellow, black and

grey, and picks up the colours that run through the apartment. The clean modern lines of the island contrast with the original architecture features in the room.

OPPOSITE The window treatments were kept very simple so as not to compete with the architectural details. The curtains match the walls and ceilings, and the fabric has a loose weave that allows daylight to shine through.

ceilings and, despite the splendour of the 19th-century architecture, the overall effect is surprisingly modern.

It's hard to believe that just a year or so ago, this tranquil, elegant interior was an impersonal, tired-looking office space with white walls and ugly modern spotlights disfiguring the tall ceilings. The apartment had been used as the headquarters of a Danish fashion brand for a couple of decades and did not have a kitchen, bathroom or any proper storage facilities. But many of the building's original features were still intact, including the wooden parquet flooring and decorative plaster ceiling mouldings, and the space still had something of

its former grandeur. It was at this point that its new owner approached Swedish design studio Note and asked for their help in transforming the apartment into a beautiful, practical family home that retained the interior's period detailing.

The Note team was headed by interior architect Susanna Wåhlin. Instead of trying to recreate a 19th-century interior, she and her colleagues decided to take it in a contemporary direction while retaining the architectural integrity of the space. One of the things that first caught Susanna's eye were the *kakelugnar* or original Swedish ceramic-tiled stoves that occupied three of the rooms in the apartment. Despite the interior's previous

OPPOSITE AND ABOVE The homeowner particularly enjoys cooking and wanted a spacious and functional kitchen. Note Design Studio were inspired by traditional Italian country kitchens, where the layout is based around various unfitted elements. The refrigerator and freezer are concealed in the freestanding khaki cupboard at one end of the room.

incarnation as an office space, the stoves had been well maintained and their distinctive glazed majolica tiles in shades of green, pink and buttery cream provided Susanna and the Note team with inspiration for a colour scheme for the rest of the home.

As work started on the apartment, other colours came to light and were added to the palette one by one, until it encompassed eight harmonious pastel tones. When a wall was demolished to provide access to plumbing pipes, it revealed an old door frame painted in a rich mustard yellow hue that has been used to adorn new storage cabinets. When the floors were sanded, beautifully patterned parquet became apparent. Each room had its own individual design and Susanna found the graphic Viennese Cross pattern of the parquet in the bedroom especially appealing. The team from Note decided to utilize its symmetrical cross pattern as a recurrent motif that would unite all the new elements in the apartment.

Wall-mounted storage cabinets were designed to hold all the necessities of everyday life and these were either made to be freestanding or attached to the walls a couple of feet up from the floor. This was to prevent any damage to the original skirting/base boards and meet the client's request that the refurbishment must respect the 19th-century splendour of the interior. The new floating cabinets are pleasingly functional and give a sense of lightness and space. All the new cabinetry features diagonal markings that mimic the pattern of the parquet flooring, as do two new walls that were constructed.

ABOVE LEFT AND RIGHT Note were responsible for choosing everything in the apartment, from paint colours to furniture to even the smallest decorative details. When it came to selecting the tableware and household utensils, they opted for contemporary shapes and textures that complemented the sophisticated colour scheme of the interior rather than the original style of the apartment.

ABOVE CENTRE The glassware collection Tela from Danish Hay has a subtle smoked colour and interesting texture that stand out against the soft yellow walls. The design was originally formed by experimenting with blowing molten glass into stitched textile bags.

OPPOSITE The splendid architectural features in this interior are its crowning glory. Built in the neo-Renaissance or Renaissance Revival style, the apartment boasts grandiose decorations such as the pediments above the doorways and the ornate plaster mouldings that adorn the cornices/crown moldings.

PAGE 114 Black details bring a little drama and definition to the tranquil decor. In the sitting room, the airy Vertigo pendant lamp by Constance Guisset for French brand Petite Friture almost seems to spread its wings and hover above the furniture. When the light is switched on, it casts elegant, attenuated shadows over the ceiling and walls.

PAGE 115 The main rooms in the apartment are arranged *en enfilade* and from the bedroom it is possible to look straight ahead through the kitchen and into the sitting room at the other end of the space. The Beetle upholstered chair and footstool from Gubi provide a vibrant pop of colour against the calm, pastel backdrop, as does the leafy plant in the foreground.

OPPOSITE In the sitting room, the furniture is arranged around the glorious *kakelugn* stove, with its rococo detailing. The quilted lounge chairs in a punchy coral shade were created by Note Design Studio for Danish brand Won. The cushioned inside of the chair was inspired by a mango fruit that has been sliced into squares before being pushed inside out. The terrazzo-topped coffee table is the Tabula, also by Note.

ABOVE The matte paint on the walls tends to absorb more light than a normal emulsion and so several contemporary lamps have been used to offer increased illumination and mood lighting. The black table lamp is the Mayfair from Spanish lighting brand Vibia.

RIGHT In Swedish bourgeois residences of the late 19th century, lavish decorative ceramic stoves were generally installed in the living room. The intricate decorative details and delicate hues of this example inspired Susanna Wåhlin of Note Design Studio to decorate the rest of the apartment in the same palette.

OPPOSITE The perfectly preserved corner stove in the bedroom is covered with majolica glazed tiles in tones of rich olive green. This type of masonry stove is very typical of the era when the house was built and is characterized by its dark tiles and their bold relief patterns. They were once to be found in almost every Swedish home, but during the early 20th century the vogue for tiled stoves slowly died out, thanks to the development of central heating and electricity.

BELOW The walls and ceilings are all painted with Pashmina paint from Swedish brand Alcro, which gives a luxurious, extremely matte effect. The wall colour in the bedroom was chosen to match the tiled stove and the green-grey tone gives the room a serene, restful mood.

RIGHT The specially designed bed is reminiscent of a Japanese futon and its angular form provides an interesting contrast to the classical ceiling rose. Like the cabinetry, the bed was built by a carpentry company that Note often collaborate with and the frame was spray-painted to achieve an immaculate finish.

For a contemporary look, in each room the walls, ceilings and mouldings were all painted the same colour, creating a calm, spacious effect. The paint used was from Swedish brand Alcro and the finish is flat with an almost velvety texture. To offer a subtle contrast, the imposing door surrounds, with their beautiful pediments and dentil mouldings, were painted a soft greenish-grey shade, as were the tall skirting/base boards, window niches and radiators.

When it came to furnishing the apartment, Note Design Studio chose modern Scandinavian designs with clean lines and simple forms, including several of their own products. The materials vary from natural unvarnished wood to powder-coated metal to sleek terrazzo.

ABOVE All the parquet floors in the apartment were sanded, then treated with a white wax oil. The upholstered pink Beetle lounge chair and footstool are from Danish brand Gubi and provide a vivid pop of colour in the otherwise tranquil green bedroom.

ABOVE RIGHT AND OPPOSITE
The walls in the study are painted a muted shade of apricot. The sofa is the upholstered Beetle from Gubi, while the floor lamp is the Silo by Note. The strong olive green of the bookshelf (seen opposite) echoes the colour of the tiled stove in the bedroom. The black desk and slender desk lamp add a little definition to the pastel scheme.

The kitchen is at the very heart of the apartment and the walls are painted a buttery light yellow. The kitchen cabinets echo the dark green hue of the tiled stove in the bedroom and feature a simple grid design on their doors. Instead of opting for classic marble, the rectangular kitchen island was crafted from functional polished terrazzo flecked with yellow, black, grey and white. Above the practical limestone splashback, Row white wall lamps from Atelier Areti were fitted to cast task light onto the worksurface, while the powder-coated Silo Trio lamp in yellow by Note hangs over the long wooden dining table.

The master bedroom is painted in a light olive green that takes its cue from the tiled stove that occupies one corner. The rest of the room has been kept deliberately simple so as not to detract from this striking feature and the ornate plaster ceiling rose. The wall behind the bed has been panelled and features the same symmetrical cross device that appears elsewhere in the apartment. In the bathroom, the gentle colour scheme and matte finishes reoccur in the form of powdery, unglazed Pico wall tiles from Italian brand Mutina. Even in here the concept is clear — calm shades, modern design and interesting textures perfectly complement the lavish period splendour of this unique apartment.

THIS PAGE The hallway is full of warmth, light and colour. The Alexandrie wallpaper from Pierre Frey features exotic vegetation and swaying palm trees, and sets the colour palette for the rest of the apartment. The wall panelling was fitted when Rikke and her fiancé renovated the apartment.

A HINT OF THE TROPICS

When interior stylist Rikke Bye Andersen moved into this period apartment in central Oslo, it was in need of some tender loving care. Over the decades, the soul of the 19th-century apartment had been eradicated by a series of refurbishments and renovations, so Rikke and her fiancé decided to restore the space to its former glory. The new parquet flooring and reinstated architectural features are faithful to the building's past, while the decor and furnishings are an eclectic mix of colours and styles. The result? A touch of the tropics in the middle of the city.

ABOVE LEFT Rikke has always loved blue and green shades and for the hall walls she chose Teresa's Green from Farrow & Ball — a warm, rich aqua blue. The finish is matte and the colour picks up those in the wallpaper. The white stoneware Dot vase comes from House Doctor DK and has an interesting irregular surface and ivory-white glaze.

ABOVE RIGHT Yellow is a recurring accent colour in Rikke's home. In the entrance hall is a low bench with a cushion covered in a vivid mustard fabric (see picture opposite), and on the kitchen countertop stands an anglepoise lamp in a lemon yellow shade. The primary colour pops against the soft pastel walls.

BELOW At one end of the kitchen stands a pretty antique wooden side table decorated with fresh flowers, books and ornamental items including a coral under a glass display bell. On the wall above hangs a portrait of Mao by Andy Warhol dating back to the early 1970s. In Rikke's home, pieces of art, textiles and small treasures contribute splashes of colour.

RIGHT In the kitchen, all the cabinets and appliances were covered with new fronts in a peppermint shade dubbed Aerugo Green from Swedish brand Superfront. This particular design is called Illusion, as its subtle pattern seems to change as light shifts during the course of the day. Some people see squares, others a zigzag pattern or box. The glossy marble worktop adds a classic element.

Located in the Majorstuen neighbourhood in western Oslo, Rikke's apartment is part of an old townhouse dating back to 1904. During the past hundred or so years, the apartment had undergone multiple renovations and most of the original architectural features had been torn out. When she first moved in, Rikke herself experimented with various different colour palettes and decorative styles, but recently she and her fiancé decided to go back to the drawing board and take on the challenge of a full restoration and refurbishment.

Visiting their neighbours gave the couple an invaluable insight into the apartment's original architecture and how it once looked. To recreate the same feel in her home, Rikke installed a *kakelugn* – a traditional tiled stove – in the living room, covered the walls of the hallway with dado-height panelling, and reinstated the cornices/ crown moldings on the ceilings. On the floors, parquet was laid in a classic Dutch pattern.

The newly refurbished apartment was decorated in a carefully chosen palette of calm pastels and furnished with a mixture of modern and retro pieces. Rikke is drawn to soft shades

THIS PAGE The kitchen and living room are open plan. Rikke opted for cool pastels here, saying that she prefers them to vibrant hues, as they create a timeless look that can be quickly updated by adding new textiles and decorative items. The pared-back decor makes the room feel lighter and draws the attention to the red dining table from Muuto and the classic CH24 Wishbone or Y-chairs by Hans J Wegner.

LEFT The living room is filled with Scandinavian design classics both old and new. The art on the wall includes works by Scandinavian artists Marit Geraldine Bostad, Johs. Bøe and Souvanni Asmussen, and harmonizes with the gentle pastel colour scheme. The large green painting is by Marit Geraldine Bostad and is entitled 'Shy but Not', which seems to sum up this soft yet colourful home perfectly.

on the walls – she feels they create a timeless backdrop that can be updated by changing decorative details, textiles and other pieces in step with different seasons and passing trends.

The apartment is full of colourful details and observant visitors will recognize several patterns by well-known 1930s designers. Rikke is greatly inspired by the classic Swedish brand Svenskt Tenn and the work of its great designers Josef Frank and Estrid Ericson. Together, Ericson and Frank transformed rigid Scandinavian functionalism into something much more inviting, joyful and vibrant. Their version of Scandinavian style was bold and sophisticated, and included pattern and colour while maintaining a sense of simplicity. The same characteristics can be seen in Rikke's home.

The public areas, such as the hallway, living room and kitchen, feature bold patterns and quirky

OPPOSITE AND LEFT Rikke and her fiancé laid new parquet floors throughout the apartment. The wood has an antique finish and a slightly matte surface treatment, which means that the colour changes in different lights. In the small home office-cum-guest room, the warm beige walls match the flooring perfectly.

LEFT For this room, Rikke chose an earthy beige hue with pinkish undertones called Soft Skin from Norwegian paint brand Jotun. Its matte finish gives a densely pigmented effect. This space doubles up as a guest room and has a calm, relaxing mood. The photos on the wall are by Esther Haase and Mikal Strøm, and their candy-coloured pastels echo the colours that Rikke has used elsewhere in the apartment.

BELOW To create a luxe hotel vibe, Rikke and her fiancé installed a small sink and mirror in the guest room — a very practical addition in a small apartment and one that allows visitors to freshen up in the privacy of their own room.

decorative pieces and are furnished with a selection of mid-century Scandinavian design classics. But this home is not all about retro styling — there is more than a smattering of contemporary art and modern furniture in organic shapes. The bedrooms are more tranquil, and are decorated and furnished with a calm simplicity.

When Rikke and her fiancé renovated the apartment, they reconfigured the kitchen and living room to create an open-plan layout that not only makes the space feel much bigger and brighter but also means it is perfect for entertaining. Lighting is important here. The sitting room boasts a Louis Poulsen Panthella floor lamp by Danish designer Verner Panton and a George Nelson Bubble Saucer pendant light that was originally inspired by a set of silk-covered Swedish hanging lamps. Over the kitchen table hangs the Semi brass pendant light from Danish brand Gubi, and the white wall lamps in the kitchen are the PH 2/1 — the smallest members of the famous PH3 family

ABOVE A notebook covered with Celotocaulis, a Josef Frank design dating back to 1930, takes pride of place on Rikke's small marble bedside table..

LEFT Both the guest room and the bedroom have built-in shelves painted the same colour as the walls. This creates a unified look and provides a soft, subtle backdrop for the cheerful items arranged on the shelves.

designed by Poul Henningsen in the 1950s. Rikke was determined she wanted to fit these lamps above the kitchen worksurface, and therefore the couple opted for roomy base cabinets rather than wall cupboards. To add colour and visual interest, they replaced the existing Ikea kitchen doors with peppermint green ones from Swedish brand Superfront, which produces new fronts especially designed to fit Ikea kitchen cabinets. This particular design is called Illusion, thanks to its subtle pattern that appears differently as light shifts during the course of the day.

Rikke runs her own company offering styling and interior design for magazines, advertising campaigns, private homes and offices. In order to stay true to her own unique sense of style, she has tried to create a home that reflects her own tastes and personality yet is neutral and timeless. It's no surprise to hear that Rikke's professional skills came in useful during the refurb – she put together detailed mood boards before the renovation got underway and she has changed the fabric on various pieces of furniture and repainted the apartment herself several times.

The result is a home that's unmistakably Scandinavian yet boasts a very up-to-date colour scheme. After more than a hundred years, this apartment has finally been restored to its former glory, but it is the colourful details that bring it to life.

THIS PAGE The bedroom is painted in Peignoir from Farrow & Ball – a soft, greyish pink shade that provides a sophisticated backdrop for the raspberry and aqua accents that spice up the room. The handmade cushions on the bed are by Danish designer Christina Lundsteen and Rikke reupholstered the Ikea headboard herself. Both thick curtains and sheer voile panels hang at the windows, allowing Rikke and her fiancé to adjust the light levels as necessary.

A SOPHISTICATED SPACE

This airy apartment with views over Stockholm has been transformed from a white, minimalist and rather impersonal space into a warm and welcoming home. When businessman Stefan Lundborg and his family decided to leave the suburbs and move back into the centre of town, they wanted a home that both lent itself to entertaining and offered a tranquil, functional base for everyday life. With the help of a calm palette, elegant furnishings and a smattering of Nordic design classics, this apartment meets their requirements perfectly.

For most parents there comes a time when little kids grow into big kids and nobody wants to kick a ball around the garden anymore. After many happy years living in Stockholm's pleasant suburbs, this happened to Stefan Lundborg, his partner and their teenage sons. The whole family yearned for the faster pace of urban life and decided to leave their comfortable suburban existence for a new start in the city centre.

In a tall 1930s house in central Stockholm, the family found an apartment that caught their attention. The huge balcony offering astonishing views over the city was a great attraction, but the modern black and white interior did not appeal. The white walls,

ABOVE LEFT AND CENTRE Sand, clay and cashmere were materials that inspired the colour palette in this apartment. The walls and ceilings are painted shades of apricot pink and sandy beige, which creates a soft, hazy atmosphere. The space works wonderfully for family life and is also great for entertaining. Stefan and his partner have demanding jobs and travel extensively, so their priority was a relaxing home that was a joy to return to.

ABOVE RIGHT The silver jug on the fireplace was inherited, while the candleholder was a gift from good friends. The latter is very appropriately called 'The Knot of Friendship' and was designed by Josef Frank for Svenskt Tenn in 1938, a year before the outbreak of the Second World War, as a symbol of peace and friendship.

THIS PAGE At first, Stefan and his wife were unsure about the pinky beige colour that covers the walls. What had looked like a soft neutral on the colour card proved to be a much more definite colour on the walls and ceilings. After a little while, and once the furniture was in place, the couple fell in love with the calming hue.

large glass partitions and black elements felt hard and inhospitable. The family decided that if they were going to make a major lifestyle change, they wanted their new home to be different and special with a spin on modern Scandinavian design.

Both Stefan and his partner work in the world of finance and travel a great deal for work. They wanted a home that was easy to live in and relaxing to come back to, but also suitable for entertaining business associates and friends from all over the world. To make their dreams a reality, Stefan contacted Stockholm-based design studio Note. The brief was to create a warm, cosy space with a homey, welcoming atmosphere and a timeless, sophisticated vibe. Note put together a mood board that attempted to capture those feelings, drawing inspiration from images of an Italian piazza, a pirouetting ballerina, a cashmere coat and a pair of sand-coloured sneakers.

ABOVE The painting hanging on the wall by the stairs is by Swedish artist and songwriter Ulf Lundell. Stefan bought it many years ago as he is a great fan of Lundell's music.

LEFT When the family moved in, there was a heavy oak staircase with glass panels leading up to the loft area. To create a neater look, it was replaced with a specially designed staircase by Note Design Studio. The new version has taller risers and is painted the same colour as the wall to blend in. The handrail is covered in a tactile leather strap.

OPPOSITE The open-plan layout contains many different social spaces, which allows the whole family to be together even while engaged with varying activities in different areas. The staircase leads up to a mezzanine level, while the spacious seating area has two long, low sofas upholstered in putty pink and sky blue arranged around the glossy Zorro table by Note.

LEFT AND ABOVE Before the apartment was renovated, there was little or no effective storage. The tall dormer windows and roof angles made it impossible to fit wall cabinets, so Note Design Studio suggested constructing low-level units holding deep drawers. These create a long horizontal line that grounds the space nicely. The warm steel blue colour reappears in the master bedroom and on shelves and doors throughout. The pale wood dining table and the gently padded Beetle chairs from Danish brand Gubi echo the soft pastel shade of the sloping ceiling.

The high ceilings, sharp roof angles and narrow dormer windows of the apartment made it difficult to use curtains to soften the space. Instead, the walls and ceilings were painted in a palette of gentle pastel hues to create a calm and composed atmosphere. The colour scheme consists of three soft shades – apricot pink, warm sandy beige and a smoky grey-blue – and painting the ceilings the same subtle colour as the walls produces a sleek, seamless effect. However, it took the family some time to get used to the results – Stefan says that the first time he and his partner saw the painted walls they were in a state of shock. Shades that had looked subtle and knocked back on the colour chart made much more of a statement when they covered all the walls and ceilings.

OPPOSITE The apartment is located in an unusually tall house in the southern part of Stockholm's centre. This means that it has magnificent views of the city and light flows in all day long. It is lovely most of the time, but can be quite confusing during midsummer, when the nights are almost non-existent, admits Stefan. The blue-grey storage units run throughout the interior and provide a strong base for the decor and the high ceilings.

LEFT The stepped staircase form is a motif that's repeated in several places – here on the side of the chimney breast. The glass vase is called Äng, which means meadow in Swedish, and is from modern Swedish design brand Klong.

BELOW Open fireplaces are a typical feature of Swedish homes and this example has a rugged, functional charm. The oak parquet flooring was sanded and treated with a little white lacquer to create a dull lustre that complements the walls.

To foster a sense of comfort and ease, the apartment is furnished with soft upholstered pieces in elegant, simple shapes. The interior plays with typical Nordic materials, a timeless colour palette and a sleek international vibe.

One of Stefan's more practical requirements was plenty of storage. The tall ceilings and awkward slanting roofs of the top-floor apartment made it difficult to construct full-height storage, so Note suggested fitting low-level, deep drawer units throughout the apartment. Painted a soft grey-blue, these units contribute a strong horizontal element that counteracts the high ceilings and adds a unifying feature to the interior.

The blue colour reappears in the master bedroom. This space was relatively small, so it was decided to enhance the feeling of intimacy and enclosure by painting the room dark blue. Stefan says the dark walls create a soothing cave-like atmosphere and, even though they live in the middle of a noisy city, the couple sleep undisturbed.

The beautiful, sculptural staircase that leads up to the mezzanine level is another feature that

THIS PAGE From this small dining area, the family enjoys views across the Stockholm rooftops. The soft beige of the walls feels even warmer when the sun shines in. The chairs are part of the Spine collection by Space Copenhagen for Fredericia Furniture. The design is influenced by Børge Mogensen but with a modern touch.

ABOVE LEFT The traditional Windsor chair has been synonymous with Swedish design since Carl Malmsten created his Lilla Åland chair in 1942 and can be found in many Swedish and Norwegian summer cottages. This version is the J110 from Hay. Its tall back and armrests create a regal, refined look, and its austere form looks striking silhouetted against the soft wall colour.

ABOVE RIGHT The blue-grey hue is picked up again on the desk, while the tan leather of the desk chair pops up throughout the apartment on details such as the the staircase handrail. The articulated black floor lamp stands ready to take over once night falls and the daylight fades away.

PAGES 140 AND 141 To create an intimate feel in the small master bedroom, the space was painted a rich, saturated steel blue. The textiles were chosen to match: the cotton bedspread is Quilt Sideways by All The Way To Paris for Hay. Plenty of effective lighting was planned to compensate for the dark walls, and the wall-mounted Bestlite lamps provide focused light to read by. The wall behind the bed is covered with a wooden panel with an incised grid design that brings the monochromatic scheme texture and visual interest.

transformed the apartment. Note replaced a large staircase with glass sections with a neat, economical flight of stairs sprayed the same colour as the walls and accompanied by slender metal banisters and a handrail covered in wound leather.

The sunlight that shines uninterrupted through the high windows also makes its mark on the interior. In the kitchen, where the family likes to meet for breakfast with coffee and the morning papers, natural light plays over the beige walls. Nowadays the family love the soft colour palette and the homey atmosphere delights guests. The open-plan layout of the interior allows them to spend time together without necessarily doing the same thing or even being in the same space – one teenage son can watch TV on the sofa while the other studies at the dining table and Stefan prepares supper in the kitchen, chatting to both of them at the same time. This is a home that perfectly balances the sophisticated and the social.

THIS PAGE Mikkel and Mette designed the house themselves, drawing inspiration from classic Danish barn architecture. The tiled chimney in the centre of the space is both beautiful and functional, as it serves to support the roof construction.

AT HOME WITH NATURE

At the northernmost edge of Zealand, Danish craftsmanship and exotic treasures
from all over the world coexist happily beneath the soaring roof of a newly built
home. The photographer Mikkel Adsbøl, his wife Mette and their two sons moved
here a few years ago, after the couple had designed the house of their dreams.
Mikkel and Mette's home exudes a very Scandinavian type of luxury. There is
no gilt or bling here. Instead, functional solutions, robust materials, a cosy
atmosphere and close proximity to nature are valued above all else.

Weary of urban life, Mikkel and Mette dreamed of a new start in the countryside north of Copenhagen. Mette had a vision of life at the water's edge, while Mikkel wanted their children to grow up surrounded by fields and woodland. The couple found the perfect plot overlooking a lake and at the edge of one of the country's largest forests, and here they built a long, low, whitewashed house inspired by traditional Danish barn architecture. The location is idyllic and the views from the house are constantly changing, depending on the season, time of day and weather.

Mikkel and Mette share a typically Nordic love of nature and this is evident both indoors and out. When they designed the

ABOVE LEFT Many of the unique decorative pieces were bought abroad and shipped back home. This old urn close to the doorway planted up with a *Monstera deliciosa* was found on a trip to France.

ABOVE CENTRE The walls of the main living area are painted Bagdad Grey — a calming blue-grey shade from Danish paint brand Flügger that was inspired by colours used in

historic Danish buildings. The piece of carved wood hanging on the hall wall was originally from a house in India.

ABOVE RIGHT For a family with children, storage is of paramount importance. The Adsbøl family planned ample storage space when they designed the house, including this long run of built-in cupboards/closets in the hallway.

ABOVE The window separating the entrance hall from the living room is more than 100 years old and was salvaged from the B&W shipyard in Copenhagen. The elegant OW150 daybed is a Danish classic designed by Ole Wanscher in 1950 and the angled brass wall lights are from Tine K.

RIGHT The kitchen was handcrafted in smoked oak by Københavns Møbelsnedkeri. Mikkel and Mette bought it before they had made a start on the house and have used the rich tones of the smoked oak as a recurrent motif. The brass pendant light was custom made.

house, the couple created mood boards and collated colour samples and materials to make it easier to visualize the final result. Their previous home was decorated in lighter tones, but in this location they decided to create a scheme based around the clear, restful blue-grey hues so often found in the Nordic landscape. Building a home from scratch allowed Mette and Mikkel to choose materials and textures in tune with the

surroundings. The floorboards are oiled ash, the kitchen is made from smoked oak and other natural materials feature throughout the interior. Each material was carefully chosen to suit the space, and the muted blue-grey walls of the home are reminiscent of foggy mornings, hazy clouds and rocky beaches.

Mikkel is a photographer and his creative eye is evident in the house's clean lines and well-balanced proportions. He admits that

he employed photographic techniques such as negative space when designing the house and that he naturally inclines towards a limited colour palette. Sticking to one main colour but using different tones on textiles, walls and woodwork has brought the space a soft, soothing atmosphere.

The calm blue shades used throughout go well with the brass details and soaring wooden ceilings in the living area and kitchen. In fact, the smoked oak kitchen sets the style for the whole house. Mikkel found it in a showroom four years before they built the house and fell in love with its rich hues, strong lines and incredible craftsmanship. The couple bought, dismantled and stored the units and then, several years later, installed them in their newly built house. Mikkel says the kitchen is one of his favourite places and he loves to cook there.

The huge exposed beams that support the roof were sourced abroad because it was impossible to find local timbers that were large enough. They have been stained a rich, dark brown to match the kitchen units and the planked roof. Mikkel adds that guests often like to knock on the timbers and to handle other objects in their home. It's as if we are fascinated with quality materials, as they are so rare nowadays.

Everything in this house was done with love and care. The walls were hand-painted and the furniture made by skilled craftsmen, while many decorative pieces were either designed by Mikkel and Mette or bought on trips around the world. The rugs came from the souk in Marrakech and the couple shipped container-loads of antiques back from India, Bali and Thailand.

When they planned the layout of the house, Mikkel and Mette divided it into two parts — an airy, sociable space that's home to the kitchen, dining area and living room, and a more intimate and relaxed zone at the other end of the barn. That feeling of cosiness and comfort is something the family want visitors to experience as well and so they planned spare bedrooms for overnight guests.

Friends warned the couple that they would miss Copenhagen and feel isolated, but they have been proved wrong. The family are happier than ever. The children play outside and love to drive an old Ferguson tractor around the plot, while Mikkel's 30-minute commute to work in Copenhagen allows him valuable thinking time every day. This home offers the best of all worlds.

OPPOSITE The floors are made of wide oiled ash planks. The eating area is home to a dining table from Koch Køkken and the chairs around the table are Hans J Wegner's CH33 and the CH26 armchair. A feeling of cosiness and comfort is highly important to the Adsbøls. They have achieved it by mixing new pieces, design classics, antiquities and finds from their travels in an eclectic mix.

LEFT Lighting often poses a challenge in a space with high ceilings. The solution here was to combine recessed spotlights with decorative fixtures at different levels. The wall lamps here are the Brass Swing Arm light by Danish brand Tine K.

ABOVE The Beni Ourain rug just glimpsed in the corner of this picture was sourced, like all the rugs in the home, in Morocco, where Mikkel and Mette bought them in the Marrakech souk. The lounge chair is the classic CH22 designed by Hans J Wegner in the 1950s.

THIS PAGE Mikkel and Mette created mood boards to ensure a balanced, coherent interior style. In front of the windows hang blue curtains that match the velvet-covered armchair from Frits Henningsen. The sofa is from Italian company Meridiani.

ABOVE LEFT The bathroom exudes unassuming luxury. The antique mirrors, taps/faucets and Bestlite wall lamps in brass stand out against the indigo blue walls. The granite sinks were shipped back to Denmark from Bali and are placed on washstands from Københavns Møbelsnedkeri. The flooring is Jura limestone containing many fossils.

LEFT The bathroom is painted in a water-resistant paint suitable for wet rooms. Mikkel and Mette initially chose a delicate powder pink colour for the bathroom, but it was recently repainted in this rich, saturated blue — a hue that emphasizes the brass details and dark wood details. The elegant hand sculpture was bought in Thailand.

ABOVE Like much of the lighting in the house, the fixtures in the bedroom were designed by Mikkel and custom made for the house. The vases were bought in Morocco and the Gustavian chair once belonged to Mette's ancestors but has been recovered in a new fabric.

OPPOSITE The calm, serene blue colour scheme links every room in the barn together. In the bedroom, the comfy feeling is amplified by all the blue textiles. The dark blue velvet curtains from Dedar block out the daylight and the soft washed linen sheets echo the hue on the wall.

SOURCES

FURNITURE

Carl Hansen & Son
www.carlhansen.com
Founded in 1905, this famous firm produces designs by Scandinavian design giants such as Hans J Wegner and Poul Kjaerholm, among others.

La Fibule
www.lafibule.fr
Luxurious contemporary furniture, sofas and lighting from a French furniture brand.

Fredericia
www.fredericia.com
Danish design house dating back to 1911 and producing many Scandinavian design classics.

Fogia
www.fogia.com
Swedish brand that collaborates with selected Scandi designers.

Gubi
Orientkaj 18–20 Nordhavn
2150 København
Denmark
+45 33 32 63 68
www.gubi.com
Designer furniture and lighting.

Hay DK
Østergade 61
1100 København K
Denmark
+45 31 64 61 33
www.hay.dk
Danish brand offering affordable designs with a modern aesthetic.

Kollekted By
Schous Plass 7
0552 Oslo
Norway
+47 400 42 743
www.kollektedby.no
Jannicke Krakvik and Alessandro D'Orazio's store in Oslo.

Meridiani
www.meridiani.it
Elegant contemporary Italian furniture from a Milan-based firm.

Muuto
www.muuto.com
Modern Scandinavian furniture, lighting and accessories, including tableware and textiles. Visit their website for your nearest stockist.

Normann Copenhagen
Niels Hemmingsens Gade 12
1153 København
Denmark
+45 35 55 44 59
www.normann-copenhagen.com
As the name suggests, a Danish design company producing furniture, lighting, kitchenware, textiles and decorative accessories.

Ochre
www.ochre.net
Beautifully crafted, elegant, contemporary lighting and furniture from a New York/ London-based British brand.

Overgaard & Dyrman
www.oandd.dk
Contemporary Danish furniture maker merging traditional craftsmanship with modern technology and sold through Rue Verte (see above), among others.

Rue Verte
Ny Østergade 11
1101 København K
Denmark
+45 33 12 55 55
www.rueverte.dk
High-end interiors store co-owned by Anders Krakau (pp. 60–69) and Michala Jessen (pp. 28–37).

LIGHTING

Artemide
www.artemide.com
Renowned Italian lighting and furniture brand.

Atelier Areti
www.atelierareti.com
European design studio producing stunning lighting designs.

Gallotti & Radice
www.gallottiradice.it
Sophisticated and luxurious Italian lighting, glassware and furnishings.

Louis Poulsen Lighting
www.louispoulsen.com
Renowned Danish lighting manufacturer producing lighting designs by iconic Scandinavian designers including Poul Henningsen and Verner Panton.

Örsjö Belysnig
www.orsjo.com
Swedish lighting brand producing exciting collaborations with Scandinavia's leading designers, including Claesson Koivisto Rune and Note Design Studio.

Restart Milano
www.restartmilano.com
Elegant minimalist furniture and lighting.

Tine K Home
Ny Østergade 25
1101 København K
Denmark
+45 71 99 33 02
www.tinekhome.com
Danish lifestyle brand offering simple, understated tableware, textiles, lighting and some very elegant furniture.

Vibia
www.vibia.com
Beautiful, dramatic and architectural lighting designs from this Spanish brand.

PAINT, WALLPAPER, FABRICS AND FLOORS

Alcro
www.alcro.se
Swedish paint brand.

Dinesen
Søtorvet 5
1371 København K
Denmark
+45 74 55 21 40
www.dinesen.com
Danish wooden flooring company producing good-quality solid oak and fir floors in a wide range of sizes and finishes.

Jotun
www.jotun.com
Norwegian paint company.

Marrakech Design
www.marrakechdesign.se
Swedish company specializing in encaustic cement tiles for walls and floors, with exclusive designs from Scandinavian designers Claesson Koivisto Rune and Mats Theselius.

Mutina
www.mutina.it
Remarkable Italian ceramic tiles designed in collaboration with leading designers.

Svenskt Tenn
Strandvägen 5
114 51 Stockholm
Sweden
+46 8 670 16 00
www.svenskttenn.com
Historic Swedish interior design company famous for Josef Frank's bold and colourful fabric designs as well as homewares, furniture, decorative pieces and jewellery.

Tapet-Café
Brogårdsvej 23
2820 Gentofte
Denmark
+45 39 65 66 30
www.tapet-café.dk

Printed textiles, wallpaper, rugs, Farrow & Ball paints, upholstery and custom-made soft furnishings. Interior design service available.

Zoffany
zoffany.sandersondesign
group.com
British paint company.

KITCHENS

Frama
www.framacph.com
Danish design studio specializing in elegant, refined furniture, lighting and a unique, freestanding low-tech kitchen system made from Douglas fir, marble, melamine and steel and designed to move house with you.

KBH Københavns Møbelsnedkeri
Sturlasgade 14
2300 København S
Denmark
+45 33 31 30 30
kobenhavns-mobelsnedkeri.com
Custom-built handmade furniture and kitchens plus a 'new classics' collection of handcrafted chairs, tables, cabinetry and lighting.

Koch Køkken
Kongevejen 340
2840 Holte
Denmark
+45 40 41 07 08
www.kochkoekken.dk
High-end Danish kitchen company producing quietly elegant handcrafted kitchens.

Puustelli Miinus
www.puustellimiinus.com
Eco-friendly Finnish kitchen company. The Miinus Kitchen is produced using ecologically friendly, non-toxic methods and has a low carbon footprint. It has great longevity and is entirely reusable and recyclable. Visit their website for details of stockists.

Superfront
www.superfront.com
Ingenious Swedish brand offering high-quality cabinet fronts, legs, knobs and handles that work with popular Ikea kitchen designs as well as the Swedish superstore's wardrobes and other storage.

DECORATIVE ITEMS AND ACCESSORIES

Bjørn Wiinblad
www.rosendahl.com/da/dk/
bjoern-wiinblad
Decorative items, ceramics and glassware created by the Danish designer and illustrator.

House Doctor DK
www.housedoctor.com
Fun, trend-led wall décor, home office supplies, storage, cushions and lighting.

Iittala
www.iittala.com
Beautiful, simple glassware from a historic Finnish company.

Rebekka Notkin
Bredgade 25A
1260 København K
Denmark
+45 33 32 02 60
www.rebekkanotkin.com
Exquisite pieces from jeweller Rebekka Notkin (see her home on pp. 50–59).

Lillian Tørlen
www.lilliantorlen.no
Norwegian ceramic artist.

PICTURE CREDITS

Front endpapers: *above centre left* The home of interior stylist Rikke Bye-Anderson in Oslo; *Above centre right* Note Design Studio; *Above right* The home of art collector Sara Lysgaard; *Below right* The home of Stefan Lundborg, designed by Note Design Studio; *Below centre right* Note Design Studio; *Below centre left* The home of Daniel Heckscher, Interior Architect at Note Design Studio, Stockholm; *Below left* House and interior designed by Mette and Mikkel Beck Adsbøl.

Back endpapers: *above left* The home of art collector Sara Lysgaard; *Above centre left* The home of interior stylist Rikke Bye-Anderson in Oslo; *Above centre right* Note Design Studio; *Below right* House and interior designed by Mette and Mikkel Beck Adsbøl; *Below centre right* Note Design Studio; *Below centre left* The home of Daniel Heckscher, Interior Architect at Note Design Studio, Stockholm; *Below left* The home of Stefan Lundborg, designed by Note Design Studio.

1 The home of interior stylist Rikke Bye-Anderson in Oslo; **2** The home of Creative Director and TV host Isabelle McAllister in Stockholm www.isabelle.se; **3** Note Design Studio; **4** House and interiors is designed by Mette and Mikkel Beck Adsbøl; **5** The home of Daniel Heckscher, Interior Architect at Note Design Studio, Stockholm; **6** The home of jewellery designer Rebekka Notkin in Copenhagen; **7** *left and right* The home of Daniel Heckscher, Interior Architect at Note Design Studio, Stockholm; **7** *centre and* **9** The home of interior designer Michala Jessen in Copenhagen www.rueverte.dk; **10–11** House and interior designed by Mette and Mikkel Beck Adsbøl; **12–13** The home of art collector Sara Lysgaard; **14** Note Design Studio; **16** Kråkvik & D'Orazio; **17** The home of interior designer Michala Jessen in Copenhagen www.rueverte.dk; **18–19** The home of jewellery designer Rebekka Notkin in Copenhagen; **20** *left* The

home of Stefan Lundborg, designed by Note Design Studio; **20** *centre* The home of interior designer Michala Jessen in Copenhagen www.rueverte.dk; **20** *right and* **21** The home of Anders Krakau interior designer at Rue Verte, Copenhagen; **22** The home of art collector Sara Lysgaard; **23** The home of Daniel Heckscher, Interior Architect at Note Design Studio, Stockholm; **24** The home of Stefan Lundborg, designed by Note Design Studio; **25** *above* The home of interior stylist Rikke Bye-Anderson in Oslo; **25** *below* House and interior designed by Mette and Mikkel Beck Adsbøl; **26–27** The home of interior designer Michala Jessen in Copenhagen www.rueverte.dk; **28–29** The home of jewellery designer Rebekka Notkin in Copenhagen; **30–37** The home of interior designer Michala Jessen in Copenhagen www.rueverte.dk; **38–49** Kråkvik and D'Orazio; **50–59** The home of jewellery designer Rebekka Notkin in Copenhagen; **60–69** The home of Anders Krakau interior designer at Rue Verte, Copenhagen; **70–71** The home of art collector Sara Lysgaard; **72–79** The home of Daniel Heckscher, Interior Architect at Note Design Studio, Stockholm; **80–91** The home of art collector Sara Lysgaard; **92–103** The home of Creative Director and TV host Isabelle McAllister in Stockholm www.isabelle.se; **104–105** The home of interior stylist Rikke Bye-Anderson in Oslo; **106–119** Note Design Studio; **120–129** The home of interior stylist Rikke Bye-Anderson in Oslo; **130–141** The home of Stefan Lundborg, designed by Note Design Studio; **142–151** House and interior designed Mette and Mikkel Beck Adsbøl; **152** Kråkvik and D'Orazio; **153** The home of jewellery designer Rebekka Notkin in Copenhagen; **154–155** The home of Creative Director and TV host Isabelle McAllister in Stockholm www.isabelle.se; **157** *above left and below right* Note Design Studio; **157** *above right* The home of Creative Director and TV host Isabelle McAllister in Stockholm www.isabelle.se; **157** *below left and* **160** The home of Daniel Heckscher, Interior Architect at Note Design Studio, Stockholm.

BUSINESS CREDITS

Mikkel Adsbøl
Interiors and food
photographer
Struenseegade 15A 1 sal tv.
2200 Copenhagen
Denmark
T: +45 51 92 57 00
E: mikkel@mikkeladsbol.dk
www.mikkeladsbol.dk
and also
www.kbhsnedkeri.dk
www.koekkenskaberne.dk
www.kmldesign.wordpress.com
www.comfortbeds.dk
Front endpapers below left, 4,
10–11, 25 below, 142–151, Back
endpapers below left.

Rikke Bye-Anderson
Interior Stylist
www.rikkesroom.blogg.no

Front endpapers above centre left, 1, 6, 25 above, 104–105, 120–129, Back endpapers centre left.

Kråkvik & D'Orazio
St Halvards gate 1C
0192 Oslo
Norway
T: +47 452 38 185
T: +47 900 72 718
E: post@krakvikdorazio.no
www.krakvikdorazio.no
Pages 16, 38–49, 152.

Miss McAllister
Creative Agency
www.isabelle.se
www.dosfamily.com
Pages 2, 92–103, 154–155, 157
above right.

Note Design Studio
Nytorgsgatan 23
116 40 Stockholm
Sweden
T: +46 (0)8 656 88 04
E: info@notedesignstudio.se
www.notedesignstudio.se
Front endpapers above centre right, below right, below centre right and below centre left, pages 3, 5, 7 left, 7 right, 14, 20 left, 23, 24, 72–79, 106–111, 130–141, 157 above left, 157 below right, 157 below left, 160, Back endpapers above centre right, below centre right, below centre left, below left.

Rebekka Notkin Jewellery
Bredgade 25
1260 Copenhagen K
Denmark
T: +45 33 32 02 60
E: RN@rebekkanotkin.com
Pages 18–19, 28–29, 50–59, 153.

Rue Verte
Ny Østergade 11
1101 Copenhagen
Denmark
T: +45 33 12 55 55
E: contact@rueverte.dk
www.rueverte.dk
Product Design:
www.arrondissement-cph.com
Pages 7 centre, 9, 17, 20 centre, 20 right, 21, 26, 27, 30–37, 60–69.

INDEX

ACKNOWLEDGMENTS

Thank you to everyone at Ryland Peters & Small for making this book so beautiful and inspirational. I am particularly grateful to Annabel, for kindly guiding me through the process, and also to Sara, for sowing the seed for this project. Beth and Sania, thank you for travelling Scandinavia and taking photographs that capture the extraordinary uniqueness of each location.

There were a few friends and family members who offered proofreading eyes along the way — my beloved Axel, Ann, Fabian, Saga and Erik, your help was invaluable.

Last but not least, I would like to thank all the homeowners for sharing their personal thoughts about colour and Scandinavian style. You have made me, and I hope many others, abandon white walls in favour of dynamic, vibrant colour.